Off the Top of My Stove

Off the Top of My Stove

Maggie Monahan

Illustrations by Helen Roberts

Taylor Publishing Company
Dallas, Texas

Designed by Deborah Jackson-Jones

Published by Taylor Publishing Company
          1550 West Mockingbird Lane
          Dallas, Texas 75235

Library of Congress Cataloging-in-Publication Data

Monahan, Maggie.
     Off the top of my stove / Maggie Monahan.
       p.   cm.
     Includes index.
     ISBN: 0-87833-618-4 : $14.95
     1. Cookery.   I. Title.
TX652.M64   1989
641.5—dc19   88-26719
                                              CIP

Printed in the United States of America

10 9 8 7 6 5 4 3 2 1

To the spirit of perseverance that dwells in each and every one of us; and to the gift of self-expression which has been given to us to complete.

Table of Contents

Acknowledgments

I wish to thank the following for their help:

My mother, who had that rare, natural ability to make it all look so easy. She seemed to cook purely by instinct, and never measured anything. As a youth, sitting there in her kitchen, I thought of her then, as I do to this day: as a magical food-fairy who threw it all into the pot, and every time, made someone happy.

My father and my two brothers, who made the art of cooking into the art of eating, always coming back for a second or third helping.

My cousin, John, a very long-distance means of support.

René DeKnight, for his unflinching faith and encouragement.

Harry Sherman, a very short-distance means of support.

Helen Roberts, for making this book come to life with her imaginative and whimsical illustrations.

Diane and Marsha Roberts, for working so consistently with Helen and me on the design of the book.

The folks at Taylor Publishing, for believing and getting the book out there.

Good food, like good friends, is one of the great celebrations of life. So come, let's all celebrate and enjoy!

Maggie Monahan

 # *Introduction*

I t's true that not everyone knows how to cook, but everyone sure knows how to eat.

The sweetest atmosphere I know of is one where appetizing aromas escape from the kitchen, filling the air and blending with the sounds of laughter . . . where "home-cookin'" includes the best of everything for family, relatives, and friends . . . where a treasure trove of riches is placed on a simple linen tablecloth, lit by faces that shine with anticipation . . . and where the highest reward is seeing it all disappear.

For me, cooking and writing about cooking are like painting a picture: completed in time, with generosity and love; like drawing a tiny dot on a high wire that suddenly becomes a bird in flight, bringing home to me more than I have given.

The simple truth here is that I wish to "underwhelm," rather than overwhelm all you cooks out there; especially all you who are soon-to-be-cooks, who have waiting before you one of the great pleasures in life—giving pleasure to someone else.

Speaking of pleasure, every now and then I think the Muses must have fun playing with me. Like leading me in and out of a situation, for what I thought were my own reasons, only to realize that, for their own reasons, it has resulted in another situation entirely; like experiencing ideas born on the wings of oregano . . .

You see, as an undiscovered playwright and lyricist, I must sometimes enter occupations which not only pay the rent, but also feed my two cats, Lulu and Rudee (until that first Broadway show hits the boards to rave reviews, of course). In the course of one such temporary vocation, I was hired to work for a top video post-production house in Hollywood. It seems they had designed a complimentary "client-kitchen" and needed someone to operate it as chief-cook-and-bottlewasher. However, they forgot to mention one small point. They had neglected to install an oven.

At first, I had my doubts about cooking for a houseful of TV producers and directors every day without the use of an oven. But, necessity being the mother of invention, before long I was delighting taste buds and being asked for my recipes. And that, in a nutshell, is how *Off the Top of My Stove* came to be.

So now, if you don't have an oven, you don't need one to create character in your cooking. And if you do have an oven, you have an alternative to using it.

I wonder which of the Muses can cook?

Maggie Monahan

Glossary of Basic Cooking Terms

C ooking well, like living well, is an acquired skill and is rarely based on assumption. With the desire to cook well comes the necessity of knowing how.

The most effective means of producing the best results in the preparation of any dish is knowing the meaning of the cooking terms in the recipe—and following the recipe exactly as written.

This listing of cooking terminology is simply designed so that you can avoid the possibility of being frustrated by a recipe, as I have been many times myself. When the recipe says to dice, what does that mean? Isn't chopping or mincing the same thing? And what's the difference between pan-broiling and pan-frying?

Take the guesswork out of cooking by referring to this glossary of the terms most frequently used in cooking "off the top of your stove."

Au jus   Meat served with its natural juices.

Batter   A mixture of flour, liquid, and other ingredients that is thin enough to pour or drop from a spoon.

Beat   To make a mixture smooth by mixing rapidly. An electric mixer, rotary beater or wire whisk may be used.

Blanch   To parboil or scald in water or steam in order to remove the skin or whiten.

Blend   To combine two or more ingredients thoroughly.

Boil   To cook in liquid at a boiling temperature. Slow boiling will cook just as effectively as rapid boiling.

Braise   To brown vegetables or meat in a small amount of hot fat, and then cover and cook over very low heat, sometimes adding a small amount of liquid.

Bread   To coat the surface of food with fine dry bread or cracker crumbs, or to coat with crumbs, then dip in diluted eggs or milk, and again coat with crumbs.

Brush   To spread melted butter or margarine or eggs, etc., on top of food with a brush.

Chill   To allow to become thoroughly cold in the refrigerator.

Chop   To cut into small pieces.

Clarify   To make clear or to separate solids from liquid.

Coat   To cover the surface of food evenly with crumbs, flour, or sugar, etc. Or to dip in slightly beaten egg or milk and then in seasoned crumbs or flour, etc.

Coddle   To simmer gently in liquid over low heat for a short time.

Cool   To let stand at room temperature until no longer warm to the touch.

Cube   To cut into small cubes.

Dash   Generally, 1/8 teaspoon of dry ingredients or liquid.

Deep-fat fry   To cook in a deep container in enough fat to cover food.

Dice   To cut into small 1/4-inch cubes.

Dissolve   To cause a dry substance to be combined with a liquid, so that the dry substance becomes a solution.

Dredge   To coat heavily with flour or sugar.

Dust   To sprinkle lightly with flour or sugar.

Flake   To break into small pieces with a fork (usually refers to fish).

Flambé   To combine food with liquor and burn with a flame.

Fricassee   Meat or fowl cut into serving pieces, cooked in liquid, and served in a thickened sauce.

GLOSSARY

Fry To cook in hot fat.

Garnish To prepare finished food for table presentation.

Glaze To coat with either a jellied or syrupy substance, either before or during cooking.

Grate To rub on a grater to produce small particles.

Grease To rub a cooking container with fat before filling with food.

Grind To put through a food processor or manual food grinder.

Julienne To cut food into narrow, lengthwise, matchlike strips.

Marinate To let food stand in a flavored mixture (marinade) to improve texture and taste.

Mash To reduce to a soft, pulpy state by beating or pressure.

Melt To reduce solids to liquids by heating.

Mince To cut or chop into very fine pieces.

Pan-broil To cook uncovered in a hot skillet, pouring off fat as it accumulates.

Pan-fry To cook in a skillet with a small amount of fat.

Parboil To boil in liquid until partially cooked.

Pare To trim or shave off the outer surface of vegetables and fruits.

Peel To strip off the outer covering of certain vegetables and fruits.

Pinch The amount of herb or spice that can be held between forefinger and thumb.

Poach To cook in simmering liquid.

Pot-roast To cook by braising, usually over direct heat.

Reduce To boil liquid over moderately high heat to lessen the amount.

Roux A mixture of melted fat and thickener used in making sauces and gravies.

Sauté To cook in a small amount of hot fat in a skillet.

Scald To dip food quickly into boiling water, or to heat to just below the boiling point.

Scramble To stir or mix gently while cooking.

Sear To brown the surface of meat quickly by very high heat.

Season To add a sprinkling of salt, pepper, or any other spice, to taste.

Shred To cut or tear into long, narrow pieces.

Simmer To cook in liquid just below the boiling point.

Snip To cut with a knife or scissors into small pieces.

Steam To cook in a closed pot with only enough water to generate steam.

Toss To lightly mix ingredients.

Wedge To cut in triangular wedge shapes.

Whip To beat rapidly with a wire whisk or rotary beater, thereby increasing volume.

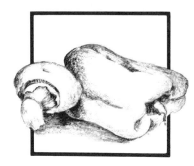

Beef
The Basics

No one can tell just by looking at a piece of meat how tender, juicy, or flavorful it will be. But when buying fresh meat, the appearance is an important key to quality.

The lean portion should be firm looking, fine grained, and bright in color, without dark streaks. The fat should be white and clear. More marbling, or flecks of fat through the lean, means more flavor and juiciness.

Generally, there are two ways to cook meat: with liquid or without. For our purposes, the dry-heat method may be used for pan-broiling and pan-frying.

Pan-broiling   Steaks may be cooked in a heavy, preheated skillet without fat or water over medium heat. Place meat in a hot skillet and turn occasionally to brown on both sides to desired degree of doneness. Pour off any fat as it collects. Season steaks after cooking.

Pan-frying   Place a small amount of fat in a heavy skillet over medium heat. When fat is melted, add steaks and cook on both sides till browned. Season steaks after cooking.

The wet or moist-heat methods of cooking include the following:

Braising   This is an excellent method for less-tender steaks or short ribs. As in pan-frying, brown the meat in a small amount of fat, and then season it. Drain off collected fat; then add a small amount of liquid of your choice (bouillon, wine, water, etc.) and any additional seasonings. Cover and cook over low heat until meat is tender.

Pot-roasting   This method works well with larger, less-tender cuts of meat. In a large Dutch oven or heavy skillet, brown the meat on all sides over medium heat. If necessary, add a little fat; then add a small amount of liquid, cover, and cook over low heat, till meat is tender.

Simmering Meats for "boiled" dinners are not browned before cooking in liquid. Wonderful, wintery meals of beef brisket, corned or fresh, are usually cooked in liquid to cover, simmering in a large kettle over low heat until tender.

*Y*esterday's brisket means a wonderful lunch for today. Just cut the meat in *thin slices, place on fresh rye bread, and top with a creamy horseradish sauce; serve with chilled coleslaw. Add some dill pickles and you'll think you're eating at The Stage Deli.*

Beef Brisket with Mustard Sauce

3 pounds fresh boneless beef brisket	2 teaspoons salt
2 medium-size onions, halved	1/4 teaspoon pepper
2 large carrots, peeled and cut into 1/2-inch rounds	10 whole cloves
	Optional: assorted vegetables
2 stalks celery, cut up	Mustard Sauce (recipe follows)

Place brisket in a large kettle or Dutch oven. Add onions, carrots, celery, salt, pepper and cloves. Add enough water to just cover beef. Simmer, covered, over low heat 3 to 4 hours, or until fork-tender. Transfer meat to a warmed serving platter. Surround meat with steamed red cabbage, cooked new potatoes and additional small whole cooked carrots. Serve with Mustard Sauce.

Serves 6 to 8

Mustard Sauce

1/3 cup dry mustard	Few grains salt
1/3 cup cider vinegar	2 tablespoons water
1 egg, beaten	2/3 cup mayonnaise
1/3 cup sugar	

Place dry mustard in a small mixing bowl. Slowly stir in vinegar and blend well. Let stand covered for a few hours. Beat egg in top of double boiler. Add sugar, salt, mustard mixture and water. Place over hot, not boiling water. Water below should not touch bottom of pan. Cook until thickened, stirring constantly. Cool thoroughly. At serving time, combine mixture with mayonnaise, using a wire whisk to blend.

A perfect compliment to this dish is Red Cabbage in Wine (p. 158). For best results, serve this vegetable in separate bowls. Add a loaf of black bread.

60-*Minute Stroganoff*

2	pounds beef top round	4	teaspoons flour
2	tablespoons vegetable oil	1/4	cup cold water
1/3	cup finely chopped onion	1/2	cup sour cream
1/2	pound mushrooms, thinly sliced	1/2	teaspoon dried dill weed, crushed
2	beef bouillon cubes	1	tablespoon flour
3/4	cup hot water	2 1/2	cups hot cooked noodles
	Freshly ground pepper		

Trim most of the fat from the meat, and cut meat into narrow strips about 1/2-inch thick. Heat oil in a heavy skillet or Dutch oven over moderately high heat. Add meat and brown pieces lightly. Remove meat; add onion and cook until tender. Reduce heat to low. Add meat, mushrooms, bouillon cubes, 3/4 cup hot water, and pepper to taste. Cover and cook 50 to 60 minutes, until meat is fork-tender. Remove meat from skillet. Blend together the 4 teaspoons flour and 1/4 cup cold water; stir into drippings in skillet and cook over moderate heat until thickened. Stir together sour cream, dill weed and flour; add this mixture to the rest of the gravy. Cook and stir constantly over low heat until sauce just starts to bubble. Add meat and heat, but do not boil. Serve over hot cooked noodles.

Serves 4

I *discovered this dish in a tiny restaurant in Chinatown. You can serve it as is, or better yet, spoon it over hot cooked rice with Spinach & Water Chestnut Toss (p. 159).*

Beefy Black Bean Short Ribs

3   pounds beef chuck short ribs, sawed
    in half across bones
2   tablespoons peanut oil
1   tablespoon dry fermented black
    bean curd
¼   cup finely chopped onion

1   tablespoon dry sherry
1   tablespoon soy sauce
1   teaspoon sugar
2   cloves garlic, minced
1   cup water

In a Dutch oven or large heavy skillet, brown ribs in hot oil, turning ribs to brown all sides. Drain excess fat, and set aside. Rinse bean curd under cold running water; drain well. Mash curd with a fork. Combine curd, onion, dry sherry, soy sauce, sugar, and garlic. Add curd mixture and water to ribs. Bring to a boil. Simmer, covered, 1½ to 2 hours or till ribs are tender. Spoon off excess fat.

Serves 4

T *he peanuts make this dish, and it's so easy to prepare. The Curried Broc-coli & Cauliflower Salad (p. 149) with a special bottle of chilled Ge-würztraminer turns a simple dinner into a memorable occasion.*

Bombay Beef

1   pound ground beef sirloin
1   tablespoon curry powder
½   teaspoon salt
2   tablespoons vegetable oil
1   cup thinly sliced onion
1   green pepper, cored, seeded, and
    cut in thin strips

½   cup seedless raisins
½   cup chopped salted peanuts
2   bay leaves
⅔   cup water
2   cups cooked hot rice

Combine ground beef, curry, and salt. Mix well. Heat oil in a skillet over moderately low heat; add onion and green pepper and cook until tender. Add ground beef mixture and cook and stir over moderate heat until lightly browned. Add raisins, nuts, bay leaves, and water. Cover and simmer over low heat for 20 minutes, stirring occasionally. Remove bay leaves and serve over rice.

Serves 4

T here's something about chili that a man just loves. Maybe it reminds him of the time when he was a little cowboy wearing his boots and holster at the OK Corral.

Gimme Gimme Chili

3	pounds ground beef chuck	5	tablespoons chili powder
3	cups chopped red onion	1	cup red wine
2	16-ounce cans whole tomatoes	1	teaspoon cayenne pepper
	16-ounce can tomato sauce	1	teaspoon sugar
	8-ounce jar salsa	12	flour tortillas
2	16-ounce cans red kidney beans *or* pinto beans		

In a large Dutch oven, place ground beef and onions. Cook over medium heat until meat is browned, and onion is tender. Drain off fat. Add tomatoes to meat. Mash tomatoes to blend in with meat. Add tomato sauce, salsa, beans, chili powder, red wine, cayenne pepper and sugar. Stir well and allow chili to simmer over low heat for an hour or longer. Spoon over heated flour tortillas.

Serves 12

S ince my parents were married on St. Patrick's Day, each year, after the parade, we would celebrate with family and friends mixed with lots of warm Irish laughter and wearin' of the green, plus plenty of cold drinks to wash down this wonderful meal.

Traditional Corned Beef & Cabbage

5	pounds corned beef brisket	2	dried bay leaves
4	cups boiling water	10	small new potatoes
1	large onion, sliced	8	large carrots
2	whole garlic cloves	2	medium-size heads of cabbage

Place beef in a large pot or Dutch oven. Cover with boiling water and add onion slices, garlic, and bay leaves. Bring water to a boil over moderately high heat, then reduce heat to a very low temperature. Cover tightly and cook for 2½ to 3 hours. Wash and peel potatoes, and halve them. Pare carrots and cut into 1-inch rounds. Wash and core cabbage and cut into wedges. Place the vegetables in with the meat, and cook for an additional 20 to 30 minutes or until vegetables are tender.

Serves 10

S ay it three times as fast as you can, and serve it with steamed bok choy on a bed of hot cooked rice.

Peter Piper Pepper Steak

1	pound beef round, cut into thin strips	1	cup green onion, sliced thin
1	clove garlic	2	stalks celery, sliced thin
¼	cup soy sauce	1	tablespoon cornstarch
1½	teaspoons grated fresh ginger *or* ½ teaspoon ground	1	cup water
¼	cup vegetable oil	2	tomatoes, cut into wedges
1	cup red *or* green pepper, cored, seeded, and cut into 1-inch squares		

With a very sharp knife, cut beef across the grain into thin strips. Combine garlic, soy sauce and ginger. Add beef. Toss and set aside. Heat oil in a large skillet. Add beef and toss over high heat until browned. Test meat. If it is not tender, continue cooking over low heat for 35 minutes. Add pepper, onion and celery to skillet and cook vegetables for 10 minutes, until crisp-tender. Mix cornstarch with water. Add to skillet; stir and cook until thickened. Add tomatoes and heat through.

Serves 4

T his Hungarian dish is also referred to as "Herdsman's Stew," and is particularly heart-warming and filling when served with goblets of Burgundy.

Goo-Goo Goulash

5	pounds boneless beef round, cut into 1½-inch cubes	4	cloves garlic, crushed
			16-ounce can tomatoes
⅓	cup vegetable oil	3	tablespoons paprika
2	tablespoons flour	1	teaspoon salt
2	beef bouillon cubes		Freshly ground pepper
2	cups water	2	12-ounce packages hot cooked broad egg noodles
3	cups onion, chopped		

Heat 2 tablespoons of the oil in a large skillet over moderately high heat, and brown meat cubes on all sides; add additional oil as needed. As meat cubes are browned, transfer them to a Dutch oven or heavy saucepan. Sprinkle meat with flour and toss to coat meat. Add beef bouillon cubes and water to skillet, and heat until meat particles are loosened. Heat the remaining ¼ cup of oil in skillet over moderate heat; cook onions and garlic until tender. Add cooked onion mixture, tomatoes, paprika, salt, and pepper to meat and stir together. Bring to a boil; cover and simmer over low heat 2½ hours, or until meat is fork-tender. Skim off fat. If desired, thin gravy with a little hot water. Serve immediately over egg noodles.

Serves 8 to 10

"Swallowing angry words is much easier than having to eat them."

English Proverb

*D*on't forget the individual bowls of chutney, raisins, shredded coconut, and peanuts, and for an added treat, salad plates of Boston lettuce, topped with mandarin orange and avocado slices with your favorite dressing.

Buddah-Belly Beef Curry

2 cloves garlic, minced	1 teaspoon sugar
1 medium-size onion, thinly sliced and separated into rings	1 teaspoon grated fresh ginger *or* ½ teaspoon ground ginger
2 tablespoons vegetable oil	Dash salt
1 pound beef round steak, cut in ½-inch pieces	Dash cayenne pepper
	1 tablespoon cold water
1 cup water	1 tablespoon cornstarch
2 tablespoons dry sherry	2 medium-size tomatoes, peeled, seeded, and chopped
1 cube beef bouillon	
2 teaspoons curry powder	

In a large skillet, cook garlic and onion in hot oil till onion is tender, but not brown. Add beef and cook quickly till all sides are browned. Drain off excess fat. Stir in the water, dry sherry, bouillon cube, curry powder, sugar, ginger, and a dash of salt and cayenne pepper. Bring to a boil and simmer, covered, 35 to 40 minutes, or until beef is tender. Slowly blend the 1 tablespoon cold water into cornstarch; stir into hot mixture. Cook and stir till thickened. Stir in tomatoes; heat through. Serve over hot cooked rice, if desired.

Serves 4

"A conversation is like a good meal. You should leave it just before you have had enough."

Anonymous

I *have heard some chili lovers from the Southwest say, "Chili ain't chili if it's* *cooked with beans." So, if you're headin' west for a chili cook-off, just hold* *the beans and kiss the judge.*

Hot 'n' Hearty Chili

5	slices bacon	3	cups water
1	chorizo sausage		12-ounce can tomato paste
4	hot Italian sausages, sliced 1-inch thick	2	jalapeño peppers, seeded and chopped
1½	pounds boneless beef chuck steak, cubed	2	tablespoons chili powder
1	cup chopped onion	½	teaspoon salt
½	cup chopped green pepper	¼	teaspoon dried oregano
1	clove garlic, minced		16-ounce can kidney beans *or* pinto beans

In a large (4 quart) Dutch oven, cook bacon till crisp; drain. Crumble bacon and set aside. Remove chorizo from casing, and together with sausage, cook till lightly browned. Add beef, onion, green pepper, and garlic. Continue cooking till beef is browned; drain off excess fat. Stir in bacon bits, water, tomato paste and jalapeño pepper, chili powder, salt and oregano. Bring to a boil and reduce heat. Cover and simmer for two hours. Stir in beans. Cover and simmer 20 minutes more or till beans are heated through.

Serves 8

T *o round out this favorite of mine, and for a tasty twist in flavor, try Cabbage* *in Mustard Sauce (p. 143) and a large bowl of Parsley New Potatoes (p. 156).* *(Double both recipes to have plenty on hand.)*

Prairie Pot Roast

2	cloves garlic, mashed	12	whole peppercorns
4	tablespoons butter *or* margarine	1	bay leaf, crumbled
4	pounds pot roast	1	tablespoon horseradish
	Flour	½	cup dry red wine
	Salt	½	cup water
1	large onion, sliced		Optional: carrots
12	whole allspice		

Sauté the garlic in 2 tablespoons of butter. Rub roast with flour and salt and brown it well on all sides. Lay the meat on the sliced onion in large Dutch oven. Add remaining butter, allspice, peppercorns, bay leaf, horseradish, and pour the red wine over the roast. Although the roast will supply most of its own juice as it cooks, pour the 1/2 cup water over it to make plenty of gravy. Cover tightly and simmer on low heat for 3 or 4 hours until the roast is tender. If you wish to serve carrots with the roast, simply add them to the pot for the last half hour of cooking. When the roast is done, place it on a round platter. Stir the gravy until smooth, and pour it over the roast.

Serves 6 to 8

With an old standby plank meal such as this, I enjoy serving the unexpected . . . so, instead of potatoes and peas, try Candied Acorn Squash (p. 144) together with Buttered Green Beans & Water Chestnuts (p. 143). Add a salad of mixed greens with marinated artichoke hearts and garbanzo beans, topped with a creamy Italian dressing.

London Broil Marinade

1/4 cup lemon juice
1/2 cup olive oil
1/4 cup wine vinegar
1 bay leaf, crumbled
1 medium-size onion, thinly sliced
1 clove garlic, crushed

1 teaspoon dried oregano
1 teaspoon salt
1/2 teaspoon pepper
2 1/2 pounds beef round steak, cut to
   1-inch thickness

Combine lemon juice, oil, vinegar, bay leaf, onion, garlic, oregano, and salt and pepper. Place meat in a large skillet; pour oil mixture over meat. Cover and let stand at room temperature for 4 hours, turning occasionally. Remove meat from marinade and drain well. Heat a large skillet over moderately high heat. Sprinkle pan with salt, and brown meat 5 to 6 minutes on both sides. Reduce heat to moderately low; cook about 10 minutes, or to the desired degree of doneness. To serve, cut across the grain into thin diagonal slices.

Serves 6

"Life is too short to be little."
Benjamin Disraeli

A dipper's delight, to serve either before the tostada or along side, is guacamole. It's easy and so good. Simply peel and mash 3 large avocados, 1 diced tomato, ½ onion chopped, the juice of one lemon, ½ teaspoon salt, and hot sauce to taste. Blend well and serve with chips. Makes 3 cups.

One-Dish Tostada

½ cup chopped onion	Vegetable oil
1 clove garlic, minced	6 10-inch flour tortillas
1 pound ground lean beef	1 large tomato, chopped
1 tablespoon cooking oil	1 small head lettuce, shredded
½ teaspoon chili powder	1 cup shredded sharp American
½ teaspoon salt	cheese
8-ounce can whole kernel corn	Creamy Dijon salad dressing *or*
8-ounce can red kidney beans	a French salad dressing

In skillet cook onion, garlic and beef in a tablespoon of oil till meat is brown and onion is tender. Drain off fat. Add chili powder and ½ teaspoon salt. Keep warm. In a saucepan, combine undrained corn and kidney beans; heat and drain. In a heavy skillet heat ¼ inch oil. Fry tortillas, one at a time, in hot oil for 20 to 30 seconds on each side till crisp and golden. Drain on paper towels. Keep warm. Place tortillas on dinner plates. For tostadas, layer the cooked ingredients equally in the following order; meat, corn/beans, tomato, lettuce, and cheese. Serve at once. Pass your choice of salad dressing.

Serves 6

"A diplomat is one who can bring home the bacon without spilling the beans."

Anonymous

16

F or an informal supper in front of the fireplace, sizzle the evening away with these little steaks plus Lobster Tails in Butter Sauce (p. 103) and a tossed green salad with a creamy ranch dressing. For wine, serve either a Beaujolais or a chilled rosé.

No-Risk Minute Steaks

2	tablespoons butter *or* margarine	1	clove garlic, crushed
1/4	cup chopped green onions with tops	2	tablespoons Worcestershire sauce
4	8-ounce minute steaks	2	tablespoons bottled steak sauce
			Freshly ground pepper

Melt butter or margarine in a skillet over moderate heat. Add onions and cook 1 minute. Place steaks in skillet and brown quickly on both sides. Remove to serving platter. Add garlic, Worcestershire sauce, and steak sauce to skillet; cook 1 to 2 minutes over moderate heat, stirring constantly. Add steaks and any meat juices to skillet. Cook about 1 minute or until steaks are cooked to desired degree of doneness. Remove steaks to serving platter and pour sauce over them.

Serves 4

T hese steaks will literally melt in your mouth, so for a little crunch serve them with French Fried Onion Rings (p. 151) and for color add South-of-the-Border Corn (p. 159) with a spinach and mushroom salad.

Killer Skillet Steaks

4	8-ounce beef rib steaks, cut 1 inch thick	1/4	cup butter *or* margarine
	Salt	1/2	teaspoon chopped fresh parsley
	Freshly ground pepper	1	teaspoon lemon juice
			Optional: watercress

Cut a few bits of fat from meat, and place in a heavy skillet over moderately low heat until fat melts. Add steaks; cook about 1½ minutes on each side for rare, or about 2 minutes on each side for medium-rare. Remove steaks to a heated platter. Season with salt and freshly ground pepper to taste. Add butter, parsley, and lemon juice to skillet; heat over moderately low heat until butter or margarine is melted. Pour mixture over steaks; garnish with watercress, if desired.

Serves 4

*A*fter you put out the bowls of popcorn and mixed nuts, and after the first round of drinks, place a tray of Fried Eggplant Straws (p. 152) on the table with a large salad bowl filled with Curried Broccoli & Cauliflower Salad (p. 149). At about half-time, bring on the sloppy joes. Your friends will cheer all the way home.

Super Bowl Sloppy Joes

1½ pounds ground beef sirloin	1 teaspoon salt
⅔ cup finely chopped onion	Freshly ground pepper
½ cup diced celery	1 tablespoon Worcestershire sauce
½ cup diced green pepper	3 hamburger buns *or* French rolls,
1 cup ketchup	split

In a large skillet, place meat, onion, celery and green pepper, and cook over medium heat until meat is browned. *Drain meat well.* Add ketchup, salt and pepper to taste and Worcestershire sauce to the cooked meat mixture. Blend all the ingredients and let cook for 15 to 20 minutes more over low to medium heat. Spoon meat mixture onto buns or crisp French rolls.

Serves 6

*O*n ski weekends, I can remember spending a lot of time in the chalet at Whiteface Mountain where you could have a bowl of something hot and watch the other skiers try to make it down from the summit.

Snowplow Steak

1½ pounds round steak, 1½ inches thick	1½ cups canned tomatoes
2 tablespoons flour	½ teaspoon prepared mustard
1 teaspoon salt	1 green pepper, seeded, and cut into thin rings
⅛ teaspoon pepper	3 medium-size onions, peeled and sliced
2 tablespoons vegetable oil	

Trim excess fat from meat; cut into serving-size pieces. Combine flour, salt, and pepper. Sprinkle one side of meat with flour, and pound it into the meat. Turn meat and repeat previous step. In a Dutch oven, brown both sides of meat in hot oil. Add tomatoes, mustard, green pepper rings, and onion. Cover; cook over low heat for 1½ to 2 hours or until meat is tender. If necessary, water may be added during cooking time.

Serves 4

*M*any centuries ago, a young princess named Sukiyaki was kidnapped by a powerful lord known as Sockittome. Together they discovered many things, including their love of good food!

Sockittome Sukiyaki

1   beef bouillon cube
½   cup boiling water
4   tablespoons soy sauce
1   tablespoon sugar
3   tablespoons peanut or vegetable oil
3   cups thinly sliced bok choy* *or* torn
      spinach
1   cup bias-sliced green onions, in
      1-inch lengths
½   cup bias-sliced celery

1   cup fresh bean sprouts
½   8-ounce can bamboo shoots,
      drained
4   large fresh mushrooms, thinly sliced
      8-ounce can sliced water chestnuts,
      drained
1   pound beef top round steak, thinly
      sliced in bite-size pieces
3   cups hot cooked rice

Dissolve beef bouillon cube in boiling water; add soy sauce and sugar. Preheat a large skillet over high heat; add oil. Add bok choy or spinach, green onions and celery. Then add bean sprouts, bamboo shoots, mushrooms, and water chestnuts; cook and stir for one minute. Remove vegetables. (Add more oil, if necessary.) Add the sliced beef to the skillet; cook and stir for 2 minutes or till meat is just browned. Stir beef bouillon mixture and add it to the beef. Cook and stir till bubbly. Add vegetables. Cover and cook 1 minute or till just heated through. Serve over hot cooked rice.

Serves 4

*Bok choy is an Oriental ingredient with large green leaves and a celery-like stalk. It may be found in the vegetable section of most markets.

B efore the great quake, there was a section in San Francisco called "The Tenderloin," an exciting district where the tips were big, and "Noodles" was the guy who collected them—ouch!

Tenderloin Tips & Noodles

6	tablespoons butter *or* margarine	1	cube beef bouillon
1½	pounds beef tenderloin tips, cut into 2-inch strips	1	cup water
		1	cup Burgundy
2	medium-size onions, chopped	1	tablespoon cornstarch
2	green peppers, cored, seeded, and chopped	10	ounces cooked egg noodles

Heat 2 tablespoons of butter or margarine in a skillet over moderately low heat; add some of the meat and brown quickly over moderately high heat. Remove meat as soon as it is browned. Add the remaining 4 tablespoons butter, as needed, to brown remaining meat. When all the meat is browned, add onion and green pepper to the skillet and cook until tender. Reduce heat to moderate; add bouillon cube and water. Combine wine and cornstarch into mixture gradually. Cook and stir about 2 minutes, until thickened. Add browned meat and heat thoroughly. Serve with cooked egg noodles and Creamy Peas & Pearl Onions (p. 148).

Serves 4

"Envy is thin because it bites, but never eats."

Spanish Proverb

Chicken
The Basics

Poultry, which includes chicken, turkey, duckling, goose, guinea hens, squab, and Cornish game hens, is an excellent source of protein. Although lower in calories than most meats, it is equal to them in protein content.

If you've been wondering which chickens are better in quality, yellow- or white-skinned; it doesn't really matter, as long as the bird is labeled Grade A and is young.

Before cooking a boneless chicken breast, pull out the white tendon that runs lengthwise through the meat, and the breast will shrink less while cooking.

If poaching a chicken for salad or other recipes calling for cooked chicken meat, let the meat cool in the poaching liquid before cutting it. It will be more flavorful, and more moist.

When buying chicken, a rule of thumb: two whole raw chicken breasts will yield about 2 cups cooked cubed or chopped chicken.

For use in your recipes, one uncooked 2½- to 3-pound fryer chicken will yield about 2½ cups cooked, chopped meat. A 3½-pound roasting chicken provides about 3 cups cooked meat.

Poultry is not only economical, but can be elegant and easy to prepare.

I can recall my mother smiling a little when someone would ask where she learned to cook such a variety of Italian dinners, and now, I find myself being asked the same question . . . and smiling a little, too.

Corky's Kitchen Chicken

½ cup flour	16-ounce can tomatoes
2 teaspoons salt	6-ounce can tomato paste
½ teaspoon pepper	½ cup water
1 3- to 4-pound broiler-fryer chicken, cut up	1 teaspoon dried basil leaves, crushed
⅓ cup olive oil	1 bay leaf
¼ cup finely chopped onion	1 teaspoon sugar
1 clove garlic, minced	¼ cup dry sherry

Place flour, salt, and pepper in a paper bag and shake well. Wash and pat chicken pieces dry. Put chicken pieces into bag, a few at a time, and shake to coat evenly. Heat olive oil in a skillet over moderately high heat; lightly brown chicken pieces on all sides. Remove chicken; add onion and garlic, and cook over moderately low heat about 5 minutes, until tender. Return chicken to skillet; add tomatoes, tomato paste, water, basil, and bay leaf. Cover and simmer over moderately low heat for 1 hour, stirring occasionally. Stir in sugar and sherry. Cook 15 minutes longer, or until fork-tender. Spoon mixture over your favorite pasta.

Serves 4 to 6

Many of my friends are half-vegetarian and half-chickenarian, so when they come over, I serve this recipe with Razzle-Dazzle Risotto (p. 81) plus Sautéed Zucchini (p. 158) and a green salad with French dressing.

Chicken a la Rudee

2-pound broiler-fryer chicken, cut up	2 cloves garlic, minced
2 tablespoons flour	½ cup dry sherry *or* dry white wine
1 teaspoon salt	8-ounce can tomato sauce
¼ teaspoon pepper	¼ pound sliced mushrooms
¼ cup butter *or* margarine	1 tablespoon chopped fresh parsley

Wash chicken pieces and pat dry. Mix flour, salt, and pepper in a paper bag. Shake chicken pieces, a few at a time, in the bag. Heat butter or margarine in a heavy skillet over moderately high heat and brown chicken, turning frequently. Add chopped garlic, sherry or white wine, tomato sauce and cook covered over moderately low heat for 30 minutes, or until chicken is fork-tender. Add mushrooms and continue to cook until mushrooms are limp. Serve sprinkled with freshly chopped parsley.

Serves 4

"Do not count your chickens before they are hatched. It is not only fine feathers that make fine birds."
Aesop

T his dish simply reeks of romance. Perhaps a New Year's Eve dinner for two, with candlelight reflecting in the flutes of champagne, and maybe a special gift given at the stroke of midnight . . . something called love.

Cornish Game Hens & Rice

2 slices bacon	1/2 cup quartered fresh mushrooms
2 1- to 1 1/2-pound Cornish game hens	1/2 cup dry white wine
Salt and pepper	1 cube chicken bouillon
1/2 cup long-grain rice	1/4 teaspoon salt
1 small onion, cut into thin wedges	1/4 teaspoon dried basil, crushed
1 clove garlic, minced	1 cup water
7 1/2-ounce can tomatoes, drained and cut up	3 tablespoons snipped parsley
	Optional: Parmesan cheese

In a large skillet, cook bacon till crisp. Drain, and reserve drippings. Crumble bacon and set aside. Tie the legs of each Cornish hen together, and twist the wing tips back. Brown Cornish hens in the reserved drippings for 10 minutes. Sprinkle with salt and pepper. Remove hens from skillet. Cook rice, onion wedges, and garlic in skillet drippings till rice is golden brown, stirring frequently. Stir in tomatoes, fresh mushrooms, 1/2 cup wine, bouillon cube, salt, basil and 1 cup water.

Bring to a boil. Return Cornish hens to skillet. Reduce heat. Cover and simmer for 45 to 60 minutes or till hens and rice are tender. Place hens on a warm serving platter. Stir parsley and crumbled bacon bits into rice; arrange rice mixture around the hens. Serve with grated Parmesan cheese, if desired.

Serves 2

F or a tasty salad, mix the torn leaves of romaine and iceberg lettuce with sliced red onion rings, sliced cucumbers, and tomatoes topped with a creamy blue cheese dressing. Add a loaf of Italian bread and a bottle of Johannisburg Riesling, clink your glasses, and pretend you're in Venice.

Double-Breasted Chicken & Zucchini

2	whole chicken breasts, skinned, boned and cut into thin strips	1	medium onion, chopped
	Freshly ground pepper to taste	¾	pound zucchini, thinly sliced
2	tablespoons vegetable oil	½	pound fresh mushrooms, sliced
2	tablespoons butter or margarine	1	cup dry white wine
1	clove garlic, minced		Juice of ½ lemon
		8	ounces cooked vermicelli

Season chicken with pepper to taste. In a large skillet, heat oil, add chicken and cook 30 minutes, until browned and tender. Remove chicken and set aside. Add butter to skillet, and cook garlic and onion till just tender, add zucchini and mushrooms, and cook over moderate heat for 3 minutes until tender. Add white wine, lemon juice, and chicken. Heat thoroughly. Serve over pasta.

Serves 4

T his mouth-watering dish is complete of and by itself, but to further enhance this meal, place washed and chilled Bibb lettuce leaves on individual salad plates and top with avocado slices, mandarin oranges, pine nuts, and a creamy Italian dressing; then fill the wine glasses with a most worthy California Chardonnay.

Chicken on the Wild Side

3	whole chicken breasts, halved lengthwise	⅓	cup wild rice, rinsed
4	tablespoons butter or margarine	⅔	cup long-grain rice
	Salt	½	cup orange juice
	14½-ounce can chicken broth	⅓	cup raisins
2	tablespoons sliced green onion	2	cups small broccoli flowerets
1	teaspoon finely shredded orange peel	1	cup sliced mushrooms
		1	tablespoon snipped parsley

In 12-inch skillet, brown chicken in butter. Sprinkle with salt. Remove chicken and set aside. Stir broth, onion, and orange peel into skillet; bring to a boil. Stir in uncooked wild rice; return to a boil. Return chicken to skillet. Reduce heat;

cover and simmer 25 minutes. Stir in uncooked long-grain rice, orange juice, and raisins; cover and simmer 20 minutes more. Stir in broccoli, mushrooms, and parsley. Cover. Cook 10 minutes or till broccoli is crisp.

Serves 6

I like to mix and match this scaloppine dish with Risotto & Chicken Livers (p. 82), and, for added taste and texture, Ratatouille (p. 157) with a simple salad of Chilled Herbed Mushrooms (p. 146).

Easy-Does-It Chicken

2	pounds raw chicken breasts, boned and sliced	2	eggs, beaten
	Salt and pepper	2½	cups seasoned bread crumbs
	Lemon juice	6	tablespoons butter *or* margarine
			Lemon wedges

Wash chicken and pat dry. Place chicken pieces between two sheets of waxed paper. Flatten pieces slightly with the side of a meat mallet. Sprinkle pieces lightly with salt and pepper. Squeeze a little lemon juice over each piece. Dip chicken pieces in egg, then in bread crumbs to coat well on both sides. Melt butter in a large skillet over moderately high heat. Fry chicken pieces until golden brown, about 3 to 4 minutes on each side. Do not overcook or chicken will become tough. Serve with lemon wedges.

Serves 4

T *his saucy chicken dish may be served with either "angel hair" pasta (Capel-lini) or rice, with Green Beans Amandine (p. 153), sesame bread sticks, and a mixed green salad with a creamy French dressing.*

Chicken Veronique

2	3-pound broiler-fryer chickens, quartered	1	tablespoon lemon juice
	Salt and pepper	1	teaspoon sugar
1/2	cup butter *or* margarine	2	tablespoons ginger
1/2	cup finely chopped onion	1	cup white seedless grapes, halved
1/4	pound sliced mushrooms	6	tablespoons water
1	clove garlic, finely chopped	1/4	cup flour
	14 1/2-ounce can chicken broth	3/4	teaspoon salt

Wash and pat chicken dry. Sprinkle chicken with salt and pepper. Melt 1/4 cup of the butter in a large skillet over moderately high heat; add chicken and cook until lightly browned on all sides. Remove chicken. Add the remaining 1/4 cup butter; cook onion, mushrooms, and garlic about 5 minutes over moderate heat until tender. Stir in broth, lemon juice, sugar, and ginger. Add chicken; cover and cook over moderately low heat 40 minutes, stirring occasionally. Add grapes and cook 5 minutes. Remove from heat. Remove chicken to serving dish. Blend flour and water together in a jar, stir into broth mixture. Cook and stir over moderately low heat until thickened. Season with salt. Serve sauce over chicken.

Serves 4 to 6

F *or some reason, the sound of chicken frying always reminds me of those cloudless, summer days in our cottage by the sea, with lots of hot, buttered corn on the cob and important conversations about which team would win the volleyball tournament, and who was supposed to bring the watermelon.*

Finger Lickin' Fried Chicken & Gravy

2	3-pound broiler-fryer chickens, cut up	2	tablespoons butter *or* margarine
2/3	cup flour	4	tablespoons shortening
1	teaspoon salt	2	cups milk

Pat the washed chicken pieces dry with paper towels. Combine flour and salt. Roll chicken pieces in flour, reserving any remaining flour for gravy. Melt butter and shortening in a large, heavy skillet over moderately high heat. When fat is hot, but not smoking, add chicken, the largest pieces first; allow room for turning. Keep skillet partly covered to avoid splatters. As chicken pieces brown, turn them. When pieces are fork-tender, drain on paper towels. Keep warm on serving platter while making gravy.

Gravy

Pour off all but 3 tablespoons of the fat in the skillet. Add 3 tablespoons of the seasoned flour and cook over moderate heat until mixture bubbles. Slowly add milk; cook and stir constantly until thickened. Continue to cook about 5 minutes. Season with salt and pepper. Serve with chicken pieces.

Serves 4 to 6

O n Sunday nights in New York City, lots of people meet for a bite to eat, and then catch an early evening movie. As a change-of-pace alternative, I like to invite friends over to enjoy good, free food and an old Bette Davis movie.

Kamikaze Chicken Wings

2	pounds chicken wings *or* drummettes		8-ounce can tomato sauce
3	tablespoons vegetable oil	2	tablespoons soy sauce
1/2	teaspoon salt	1	teaspoon freshly grated ginger
1	teaspoon cayenne pepper	2	tablespoons cornstarch
2	chicken bouillon cubes	2	tablespoons water
2	cups boiling water	2	cups cooked rice
1/2	cup sliced green onion		Chopped fresh parsley

Wash and pat chicken wings or drummettes dry. Heat oil in a large skillet over moderately high heat. Add chicken and cook on all sides until browned, turning occasionally. Sprinkle with salt and cayenne pepper. Dissolve chicken bouillon cubes in the boiling water. Pour liquid over wings in the skillet. Reduce heat to moderately low; cover and simmer 45 minutes, or until chicken is tender. Add onion and tomato sauce. Stir to blend well, and simmer 5 minutes. In a small bowl, combine soy sauce, ginger, cornstarch, and water and blend well. Gradually pour into skillet, stirring constantly until mixture is thickened and smooth. Serve with cooked rice, garnish with parsley.

Serves 4

For an appetizer at this dinner party, serve up a platter of Spicy Spareribs (p. 72) with little bowls of Chinese mustard and duck sauce for dipping. Don't forget the chopsticks and fortune cookies!

Yum-Yum Chicken & Vegetables

1½ pounds whole chicken breasts, skinned, halved lengthwise, boned, and cut into thin strips
3 tablespoons soy sauce
1 tablespoon cornstarch
½ cup cold water
2 teaspoons dry sherry
1 teaspoon fresh grated ginger
3 tablespoons cooking oil
4 green onions, sliced on the bias into 1-inch lengths

½ pound fresh mushrooms, sliced
½ 8-ounce can bamboo shoots, drained
1 cup chopped celery
8-ounce can sliced water chestnuts
½ cup chopped walnuts
1 cup frozen peas, thawed
2 tablespoons peanut oil
3 cups cooked rice

Cut chicken into thin strips and set aside. In small bowl combine soy sauce, cornstarch, water; stir in the dry sherry and ginger. Preheat a large skillet over high heat; add cooking oil. Stir-fry the green onions in hot oil for 2 minutes or till crisp tender. Remove from skillet. Add the mushrooms and bamboo shoots with the celery and sliced water chestnuts. Stir-fry for 1 or 2 minutes. Remove from skillet. Add walnuts to the skillet, adding more oil if necessary, and stir-fry for 1 or 2 minutes until golden. Remove from skillet. Add half of chicken to hot skillet, stir-fry 2 minutes. Remove from skillet. Stir-fry remaining chicken for 2 minutes. Return all chicken to skillet. Stir in soy mixture; stir into chicken. Cook and stir till thickened and bubbly. Stir in the onion, mushrooms, bamboo shoots, celery, water chestnuts, walnuts, and peas. Cover and cook 1 minute more. Serve over rice.

Serves 6

*"Many a good man has failed
Because he had his wishbone
Where his backbone should have been."*

Anonymous

T his tried-and-true Oriental recipe is a favorite of mine; it is delightful when served with a plum wine and a simple side dish of thinly sliced cucumbers vinaigrette, topped with toasted sesame seeds.

Moo Goo Gai Pan

2	tablespoons cornstarch	1/4	teaspoon garlic powder
1/2	teaspoon salt	1/4	teaspoon ground ginger
2	whole, boned, skinned, and cubed chicken breasts	1	tablespoon soy sauce
		1	tablespoon dry sherry
3	tablespoons vegetable oil		14 1/2-ounce can chicken broth
2	green onions, cut on the bias	1	package frozen Chinese pea pods
1/4	pound fresh mushrooms, sliced	2	cups cooked rice

In a medium-size bowl, combine 1 tablespoon of the cornstarch and the salt. Place chicken in bowl with cornstarch and toss lightly to coat pieces well. Heat oil in a large skillet. Add chicken pieces and cook, stirring constantly, until chicken is done and lightly browned, about 3 to 4 minutes. Remove chicken; add the onions, mushrooms, garlic powder, and ginger. Cook, stirring occasionally, for about 1 minute. In a small bowl, combine soy sauce, sherry, and the remaining 1 tablespoon cornstarch and blend well. Stir chicken broth into skillet, add cornstarch mixture gradually, stirring constantly, and cook until mixture thickens. Stir in pea pods. Simmer 30 seconds. Stir in chicken. Cook a few minutes until thoroughly heated. Serve over rice.

Serves 4

T hese tasty tidbits have proven to be an all-time favorite at my Friday all-night poker get-togethers. Of course, have lots of napkins on hand — or play with a washable deck of cards.

Sesame Seed Chicken Drummettes

¼ cup sugar	2 eggs, beaten
¼ cup flour	2 cloves garlic, minced
½ cup cornstarch	2 tablespoons sesame seeds
5 tablespoons soy sauce	Vegetable oil
1½ teaspoons salt	3 pounds chicken drummettes
2 green onions, sliced	

Combine sugar, flour, cornstarch, soy sauce, salt, green onions, beaten eggs, garlic, and sesame seeds in a bowl. Stir in ¼ cup oil. Place chicken drumettes in mixture and marinate overnight. In a large skillet, heat oil and fry drummettes a few at a time, until golden brown.

Serves 6

A subtle surprise combination with these tasty chicken livers is to heap them over cooked farfalle (butterfly pasta) and a salad of Chilled Green Beans à la Niçoise (p. 146). This menu blends an unusual mix of flavors and is perfect for a late brunch or early dinner get-together.

Savory Chicken Livers

2 tablespoons butter or margarine	Pinch dried rosemary leaves, crushed
1 pound chicken livers	Dash of pepper
2 chicken bouillon cubes	1 tablespoon cornstarch
1½ cups boiling water	2 tablespoons water
½ pound sliced mushrooms	
½ teaspoon salt	

Heat butter in a skillet over moderate heat. Add chicken livers and cook until lightly browned, turning frequently. Dissolve bouillon cubes in the boiling water. Add bouillon, mushrooms, salt, rosemary, and pepper to livers. Cover and cook over moderately low heat for 10 minutes, or until chicken livers are cooked through. Mix cornstarch and 2 tablespoons water together and stir into liquid in pan; cook 5 minutes, stirring constantly.

Serves 4

A tasty combination of flavors, serve the chicken with Sunny Risotto Lemonese (p. 80) and Chilled Green Beans à la Niçoise (p. 146). For a light dessert, serve a fruit cup of chunks of Crenshaw melon and fresh pineapple, topped with sliced bananas.

Lemon-Fricasseed Chicken

2 2½-pound broiler-fryer chickens, cut into pieces	4 tablespoons flour
Salt and pepper	2 chicken bouillon cubes
¼ cup olive oil	1½ cups boiling water
¼ cup butter *or* margarine	1 cup dry white wine
1 clove of garlic, quartered	⅓ cup lemon juice
	¼ cup chopped parsley

Wash chicken pieces and dry on paper towels. Sprinkle with salt and pepper. Put olive oil, butter or margarine, and garlic slices in a large heavy skillet and heat. Add chicken and lightly brown on all sides over moderately high heat. Cover and cook 35 minutes or until fork-tender. Remove chicken pieces. Pour or spoon off excess fat from the skillet. Reduce heat to moderate. Blend flour into drippings in skillet. Dissolve chicken bouillon cubes in boiling water and add gradually to skillet. Add wine and lemon juice, stirring to blend. Cook, stirring constantly, until thickened and smooth. Add chicken pieces to gravy and simmer a few minutes to heat through. Arrange chicken on a serving platter. Sprinkle with chopped parsley, and serve with extra gravy.

Serves 4 to 6

"What is sauce for the goose may be sauce for the gander, but not necessarily sauce for the chicken, the duck, the turkey or the guinea hen."
Alice B. Toklas

Eggs
The Basics

T he egg . . . the eighth wonder of the world!

Here is a food staple that defies the imagination. The egg makes fine bread crumbs cling to a piece of meat, it makes oil and water mix, and it raises to heaven the lightest of angel cakes.

From the moment my mother served me a boiled egg in a little egg cup, I knew my destiny was sealed, and that each new tomorrow would begin with *The Egg and I.*

In time, I have found that an egg should be thought of as fragile and temperamental about temperature. To preserve quality, eggs must be stored in the refrigerator, and should be put away promptly when you unpack your groceries.

Even out of the shell, eggs must be treated tenderly. They are delicate objects and should always be cooked gently over low or moderate heat. Eggs cooked over high heat become rubbery, lose their flavor, and are difficult to digest.

The following are a few tricks I've learned in preparing eggs, together with some basic ways to prepare one of nature's smallest wonders.

A tablespoon of vinegar added to water before poaching eggs helps to keep the whites from spreading.

For scrambled eggs and omelets, try lacing them with dry sherry. Beat it into the eggs before you cook them.

When you hard-boil eggs for stuffing, gently swizzle them in the water for the first 2 minutes. This action will set the whites. The yolks will be in the center, leaving a strong circumference of white around the yolk that won't break when the eggs are stuffed.

To prevent an egg from cracking when it's placed in boiling water, puncture the broad end with a sharp needle.

When an egg has been hard-boiled, its appearance does not change. So to tell the difference, spin the egg on its side. If it wobbles, it's uncooked; a cooked egg will spin smoothly.

Hard-boiled eggs will peel more easily if, immediately after cooking, you plunge them into a bowl of cold water. Then crack the eggs gently all over and let them remain in the water until cooled.

If you're not sure just how fresh an egg is, put it in a deep container of cold water. If it floats to the top, it's too old to use.

There are some aspiring cooks out there about whom you may have heard others say, "She can't even boil an egg!"

So to avoid this fate, note the following important, *basic* ways to prepare eggs for use in the recipes in this chapter.

To fry   (for two eggs) In a skillet over moderate heat, heat 1 tablespoon of butter or margarine until it sizzles. Break and slip eggs, from a sauce dish if you prefer, into the hot skillet. Cook slowly 3 or 4 minutes to desired doneness. For sunny-side-up eggs, baste with butter or margarine or cover skillet tightly during cooking. If you prefer eggs fried over, flip the eggs with a broad spatula, being careful not to break the yolk, and let them cook briefly on the other side.

To soft-cook   There are two basic methods for cooking eggs in the shell: using either cold water or the boiling-water method. It's easier and quicker to use the cold-water method because eggs can be taken directly from the refrigerator and put into the cooking pot without the risk of cracking shells.

To cook eggs in cold water, put them in a saucepan deep enough to hold them without crowding, and add enough cold water to cover. Bring to a boil, uncovered. Turn off heat; set pan off burner, cover, and let stand 2 to 4 minutes, depending on how firm or soft you like your eggs. Cool eggs at once in cold water to prevent further cooking.

To hard-cook   Again, for the cold-water method, follow the same procedure as soft cook, except allow the eggs to stand 15 minutes after you remove them from the heat. After the 15 minutes, plunge them immediately into cold water. This makes the shells easier to remove and prevents the yolks from discoloring on the surface.

To store shelled eggs   Shelled hard-cooked eggs may be stored, covered, in the refrigerator for no more than two days.

To poach   For best results, use only fresh eggs. Fill a shallow pan or skillet three-fourths full of water—it should be at least two inches deep. Bring water to a boil over moderately high heat, then reduce the heat to simmering. Break each egg separately into a saucer or sauce dish; bring the rim of the dish to touch water, and tilt to slip the egg quickly and gently into the water. Cook 3 to 5 minutes, depending upon the firmness desired. Serve immediately on toast or muffins.

To scramble   Allow two eggs per serving, and cook over low heat in butter or margarine. Start by breaking the required number of eggs into a bowl and blending the eggs well with a fork. Add salt and pepper and any other herbs or seasonings you desire. Add 1 tablespoon of milk per egg, and blend it in. Heat the butter or margarine in the skillet, and pour in the egg mixture. As the mixture begins to thicken, lift the cooked portion from bottom and sides, allowing the thin, uncooked portion to flow to the bottom of the pan. Avoid constant stirring. Cook about 5 to 8 minutes, until eggs are firm but moist throughout.

W hen you have colored two dozen eggs for Easter Sunday, and everyone has ooohed and aaahed and taken one home, what do you do with the ones still sitting on the dining room table? Just chill 'em, then stuff 'em, then eat 'em!

Easter Stuffed Eggs

6	hard-cooked eggs	1	tablespoon finely chopped pimento
2	tablespoons chopped toasted almonds	1/8	teaspoon hot sauce
		3	tablespoons mayonnaise
1	tablespoon minced green pepper	1/4	teaspoon salt
1	teaspoon grated onion	1/4	teaspoon pepper

Cut eggs in half lengthwise; remove yolks and press them through a fine sieve. Add remaining ingredients. Mix well. Fill egg-white halves with this mixture. Chill if desired.

Serves 6

W hat an elegant Sunday brunch! Just add a pretty basket of warm buns or assorted rolls, two different jellies, and sliced melon with fresh strawberries. Top off with chilled glasses of your favorite champagne.

Cheesy Asparagus Omelet

1/2 pound asparagus, bias-sliced into 1-inch pieces	1/4 teaspoon salt
6 eggs	Dash white pepper
2 tablespoons water	2 tablespoons butter or margarine
	Optional: paprika

Cook cut-up fresh asparagus in a small amount of boiling water until crisp-tender, or about 8 to 10 minutes. Drain and keep warm. Beat eggs with 2 tablespoons water, salt, and pepper using a fork, till well-blended. In a 10-inch skillet or omelet pan, heat butter or margarine until it browns and sizzles slightly. Tilt pan to grease sides. Add egg mixture and cook slowly. Run spatula around edges to lift the egg and allow the uncooked mixture to flow underneath. Spoon cooked asparagus across center of omelet; top with 1/2 cup Cheesy Sauce. Tilt pan to fold omelet and roll onto hot platter. Serve with remaining Cheesy Sauce, and top with paprika, if desired.

Serves 4

Cheesy Sauce

1/4 cup butter or margarine	2 cups milk
1/4 cup flour	1 teaspoon prepared mustard
1 teaspoon salt	1/2 pound shredded American cheese
1/4 teaspoon pepper	

Melt butter in a small saucepan over moderately low heat; blend in flour, salt, and pepper. Gradually add milk and cook, stirring constantly, until thickened and smooth. Add mustard and cheese. Stir until cheese melts. Do not boil.

"There is no such thing as a pretty good omelet."

French Proverb

I can smell the coffee brewing and the bacon sizzling on the stove. It reminds me of those rainy Saturday mornings in New York when we would have a leisurely breakfast before venturing out to Bloomingdale's.

Off-the-Wall Eggs

¼	cup butter *or* margarine	1	teaspoon prepared mustard
¼	cup flour	2	cups sharp Cheddar cheese
1	teaspoon salt	8	hard-cooked eggs
¼	teaspoon pepper	8	slices toast
2	cups milk		Paprika

Melt butter in a small saucepan over moderately low heat; blend in flour, salt, and pepper. Gradually add milk and cook, stirring constantly, until thickened and smooth. Add mustard and cheese. Stir until cheese is melted. Cut eggs in half lengthwise. Arrange two halves on each slice of toast. Top with cheese sauce. Sprinkle with paprika.

Serves 4

A dd a serving of Hashed-Brown Potatoes (p. 155) and sliced tomatoes to each plate, and cups of freshly brewed coffee. Then relax and enjoy the rest of the day doing the "Times" crossword puzzle.

Eggs with Tarragon-Mushroom Sauce

8	hard-cooked eggs, sliced	1½	cups milk
2	tablespoons butter *or* margarine	½	teaspoon dried tarragon leaves, crushed
1	medium onion, thinly sliced		
2	tablespoons flour	½	cup dry white wine
½	teaspoon salt	6	small mushrooms, sliced
½	teaspoon pepper		Toast

Arrange sliced eggs on serving plate. Melt butter in a medium-size saucepan over moderately low heat; sauté onions till tender. Remove onions. Add more butter, if necessary, to blend flour, salt, and pepper, beating constantly with wooden spoon to prevent lumping. Gradually add milk, stirring constantly, until sauce thickens and comes to a boil. Blend in the tarragon and onions. Gradually add wine, stirring well. Stir in mushrooms and heat through thoroughly. Serve hot sauce over sliced eggs on toast.

Serves 4

W ith this saucy dish, I prefer a pretty bowl of freshly made fruit salad. Throw in sliced peaches, watermelon, seedless red grapes, cantaloupe, kiwi, chopped walnuts, toss, and top with kirsch.

Poached Eggs Benedict

4 English muffins
   Butter *or* margarine
8 thin slices of boiled ham *or* 8 slices
   of Canadian bacon

8 eggs
1 cup Hollandaise Sauce

Hollandaise Sauce

1 cup (2 sticks) sweet butter
3 egg yolks
3 tablespoons lemon juice

½ teaspoon salt
   Few grains cayenne pepper

Before poaching eggs prepare hollandaise sauce as follows: Place butter in a small saucepan over moderately low heat until bubbling hot. Put egg yolks, lemon juice, salt, and cayenne pepper in blender; cover, and switch on and off to blend. With motor at high speed, gradually add hot butter in a steady stream until all butter is added. Turn off at once. Serve immediately or place hollandaise in saucepan over hot water to keep warm.

Split English muffins; lightly toast and butter each half. Fry ham or bacon until lightly browned. Meanwhile, poach eggs in salted water. Arrange 2 muffin halves, buttered side up, on plate. Put a slice of ham or bacon on each muffin half; put a poached egg on ham. Spoon hollandaise sauce over eggs.

Serves 4

"A boiled egg raised its little lid
And revealed its buttercup yolk."

Colette

T his regional dish may also be served mounted on a thick slice of cooked ham or Canadian bacon.

French Poached Eggs

1	large onion sliced	1/2	cup light cream
	Chicken stock	1	egg yolk
4	slices French bread (cut thick)	4	eggs
	Butter	1/2	teaspoon salt
4	cooked mushroom caps, quartered	1/4	teaspoon pepper

Simmer onions in chicken stock—enough to just cover. While onions are simmering, fry bread on both sides in a little bit of butter. When onions are tender, add mushroom caps and cream beaten with egg yolk. Poach eggs. Season sauce with salt and pepper and stir until slightly thickened. *Do not boil.* Place a poached egg on each piece of bread and spoon sauce over each. Serve immediately.

Serves 4

> *"Man has his will, but woman has her way."*
>
> Oliver Wendell Holmes

A frittata is an open-faced omelet that's perfect for quick meals and works with all kinds of fillings. This frittata may be served for supper with simple skillet-cooked lamb chops, accompanied by Summer Squash Medley (p. 160).

Potato-Onion Frittata

1/3	cup olive oil *or* vegetable oil	1/4	cup Parmesan cheese
3	cups thinly sliced potatoes	2	tablespoons snipped parsley
1/2	cup chopped onion	1/4	teaspoon salt
	Salt and pepper		Dash cayenne pepper
6	beaten eggs		

In a 10-inch skillet, heat oil. Add potatoes and onion, stir to coat with oil. Sprinkle with a little salt and pepper. Cover; cook over medium-low heat about 10 minutes or till potatoes are tender and browned; lift and turn occasionally with spatula. Combine eggs and remaining ingredients; pour over potatoes. Cover; cook over low heat about 10 minutes or till eggs are set but still glossy. Loosen egg and potato mixture; cut into wedges.

Serves 4 to 6 as side dish

T *here's a variety of ways to serve this brunch idea. Spoon the mixture into cooked, scooped-out Idaho potato shells; serve on a bed of cooked spinach; or very simply, spoon over toasted slices of rye bread.*

Scalloped Ham & Eggs

4	medium-size onions, thinly sliced	1/4	teaspoon pepper
3	tablespoons butter *or* margarine	1 1/2	cups milk
2	tablespoons flour		4 1/2-ounce can deviled ham
1/4	teaspoon salt	6	hard-cooked eggs, cut into eighths

Fry onions in butter in skillet over moderate heat until tender. Blend in flour, salt and pepper. Gradually add milk and cook 5 minutes; constantly stir until mixture is thick. Blend in ham and eggs. Cover for additional 3 minutes until set.

Serves 4

A *delightful dish for brunch, lunch, or a light dinner, served with a basket of fresh muffins and rolls, individual bowls of Chilled Herbed Mushrooms (p. 146) and a frosty bottle of champagne.*

Spinach Frittata

1	tablespoon butter *or* margarine	1/2	cup fontina cheese, shredded
2	tablespoons chopped onion	1/4	teaspoon salt
1	small clove garlic, minced		Pinch ground nutmeg
1/2	pound fresh spinach, stems removed, and chopped, *or* 1/2 10-ounce package frozen chopped spinach, thawed		Pinch pepper
		6	beaten eggs

In a saucepan, melt 1 tablespoon butter or margarine. Add onion, garlic, and fresh or thawed spinach. Cook over medium heat, stirring frequently, for about 15 minutes or until liquid is evaporated from spinach. Remove from heat; stir in cheese, salt, nutmeg, and pepper. Combine eggs and spinach mixture. Cover and cook for 3 minutes. As eggs set, run a spatula around edge of skillet, lifting egg mixture to allow uncooked portion to flow underneath. Continue cooking and lifting edges until almost set. Cover again, for 2 minutes, until the top is set. Sprinkle with additional shredded fontina cheese, if desired.

Serves 4

S erve this frittata with hot, buttered flour tortillas and a chilled pitcher of white wine sangria.

Spanish Frittata

2 large potatoes, peeled and finely chopped	2 medium tomatoes, finely chopped
1 medium onion, finely chopped	6 beaten eggs
¾ teaspoon salt	⅓ cup milk
¼ teaspoon crushed red pepper flakes	½ teaspoon salt
2 tablespoons vegetable oil	Freshly ground pepper

Combine potatoes, onion, ¾ teaspoon salt, and crushed red pepper flakes. Heat oil in a 10-inch skillet. Add potato mixture to skillet; cover and cook over medium heat 12 to 15 minutes or till tender, stirring occasionally. Combine tomatoes, eggs, milk, salt, and pepper and pour over potatoes in skillet. Reduce heat; cover and cook over low heat 8 to 12 minutes or till eggs are set.

Serves 4 to 6

T his combination develops into a Mexican dish when served over warmed, buttered flour tortillas, with a sprinkling of salsa and slices of avocado.

Sausage & Eggs

3 Italian sweet sausages	Pinch pepper
8 eggs	1 medium tomato, peeled, seeded, and chopped
¼ cup milk	
¼ teaspoon salt	

Remove casing from sausage, and crumble into an unheated 10-inch skillet. Slowly cook sausage for 15 to 20 minutes, stirring occasionally. Drain off excess fat. In a bowl, beat eggs, milk, salt, and pepper with a fork.

Pour egg mixture over sausage in skillet. Cook without stirring over low heat till eggs start to set on bottom and sides of pan. Lift and fold eggs with spatula so uncooked part runs to bottom. Continue lifting and folding for 2 or 3 minutes or till eggs start to set. Fold in the chopped tomato. Continue lifting and folding 2 to 3 minutes more or till eggs are cooked through, but still glossy and moist.

Serves 4

Lamb
The Basics

L amb is the meat of a young sheep. It is tender and flavorful, and a delightful change of pace from beef and pork.

Lamb, for the most part, lends itself to the dry-heat or oven method of cooking.

However, for the purposes of *Off-the-Top-of-My-Stove* cooking, I've discovered that there are still some lamb skillet dishes that are interesting in their simplicity and yet stand shoulder-high with the more traditional roasted leg of lamb.

S *poon some of the sauce over steamed asparagus and serve with Fried Sweet Potatoes (p. 153) and a tossed green salad.*

Braised Shoulder Lamb Chops

1/4 cup vegetable oil	1/4 teaspoon dried marjoram leaves
1 medium onion, sliced	1/4 teaspoon pepper
6 shoulder lamb chops, 3/4 inch thick	10 1/2-ounce can condensed golden
1 cup hot water	mushroom soup, undiluted
1 beef bouillon cube	

Heat oil in a large skillet over moderate heat; add onion and cook until lightly browned. Remove onion. Add chops and brown well on both sides over high heat. Remove chops and drain off any excess fat. Return skillet to heat and reduce heat to low; stir in hot water, bouillon cube, marjoram, and pepper. Stir to loosen browned bits on the bottom of skillet. Return chops and onion to the skillet with the mushroom soup. Cover and simmer 50 minutes, or until chops are fork-tender. Remove cover and simmer 10 minutes longer.

Serves 6

R *ound out this meal-in-one with Asparagus Vinaigrette (p. 140) and a basket of warm dinner rolls.*

Citrus Lamb & Rice Skillet

1 clove garlic, minced	½ teaspoon ground cinnamon
1½ pounds of boneless lamb, cut into 1-inch pieces	1 cup water
3 tablespoons vegetable oil	1 medium green pepper, cut into strips
½ cup sliced onion	11-ounce can mandarin orange sections, drained
¾ cup uncooked brown rice	Handful of snipped parsley
1 cup orange juice	
1 chicken bouillon cube	

Brown garlic and lamb in oil in a large skillet. Remove lamb; set aside. Add onion to skillet; cook until tender. Stir in uncooked brown rice. Continue cooking 5 minutes; stir frequently. Return lamb to skillet. Stir in orange juice, bouillon cube, cinnamon, and 1 cup of water. Bring to a boil; reduce heat. Cover; simmer 30 minutes. Add green pepper. Simmer, covered, 30 minutes more or till lamb and rice are tender and liquid is absorbed. Stir in oranges; heat through. Sprinkle with parsley.

Serves 6

> *"A sharp tongue is the only edged tool that grows keener with constant use."*
> Washington Irving

I *wonder if anyone has ever thought of making a curry-scented air freshener?*

Hootchie-Cootchie Curry

1½ pounds lean lamb shoulder, cut into 1-inch cubes	1 medium onion, sliced
Few grains pepper	¼ cup flour
1 teaspoon salt	2 teaspoons curry powder
¼ teaspoon cumin seed	2 cups milk
1 bay leaf	½ cup shredded green apple
1½ cups water	¼ cup golden raisins
¼ cup butter *or* margarine	2 cups hot cooked rice
	Fresh parsley

Combine lamb, pepper, ½ teaspoon of the salt, cumin seed, bay leaf, and water in a large saucepan. Place over moderate heat and bring to a boil. Reduce heat to low; cover and simmer 1½ hours, or until lamb is fork-tender.

Remove lamb and strain liquid; skim off fat. There should be ½ cup liquid left. Set liquid aside. Melt butter and cook onion until crisp-tender. In the same saucepan, quickly stir in flour, the remaining ½ teaspoon salt, and curry powder. Remove from heat and gradually stir in milk and ½ cup stock. Return to heat; bring to a boil and boil 1 minute, stirring constantly. Add apple, raisins, and cooked lamb. Heat to serving temperature, stirring constantly. Serve over cooked rice. Garnish with parsley.

Serves 4

*B*ecause of the many flavors that go into this dish, it is best served with buttered brown rice and a simple salad of Chilled Herbed Mushrooms (p. 146).

Lamb Paprikash

2	pounds boneless lamb, cut into 1-inch pieces	4	medium potatoes, peeled and quartered
1	clove garlic, minced	2	medium parsnips, sliced
2	tablespoons olive oil	2	medium carrots, sliced
3	teaspoons paprika	1	small onion, sliced
1	chicken bouillon cube	1	medium green pepper, chopped
½	teaspoon salt	1	cup sour cream
⅛	teaspoon pepper	2	tablespoons all-purpose flour
1¼	cups apple juice	2	tablespoons snipped parsley

In a large skillet, cook lamb and garlic in hot oil till lamb is browned. Drain off fat. Combine paprika, bouillon cube, ½ teaspoon salt, and ⅛ teaspoon pepper; sprinkle over lamb. Pour apple juice over all. Bring to a boil; reduce heat. Cover; simmer 15 minutes. Add next 5 ingredients. Cover; simmer 30 minutes or till vegetables are done. Combine sour cream and flour. Push lamb and the vegetables to one side of skillet. Stir sour cream mixture into liquid in skillet; blend well. Cook and stir till thickened and bubbly. Sprinkle with parsley.

Serves 6

G ood friends, French bread and Burgundy make this a very special meal indeed.

Lamb Pot Roast

4 pounds lamb shoulder, boned, rolled and tied
1 garlic clove
2 tablespoons flour
2 teaspoons salt
1/4 teaspoon pepper

3 tablespoons vegetable oil
1/2 cup water *or* beef bouillon
6 large potatoes, peeled and quartered
4 large carrots, chunky-cut

Rub meat with cut side of garlic. Combine flour, salt and pepper. Rub outside of meat with this mixture. Heat oil in heavy saucepan or Dutch oven over moderately high heat. Turn meat to brown on all sides. Add water or bouillon. Cover tightly; cook over low heat for about 3 hours until lamb is fork-tender. Add a little more water if necessary. Add potatoes and carrots during the last hour of cooking.

Serves 6 to 8

W hile this dish is cooking gently—and filling the house with appetizing smells—seat your guests for a most worthy treat: French-Dip Artichokes (p. 151).

Skillet Mushrooms & Lamb

3 tablespoons butter *or* margarine
1 pound lean boneless lamb, cut into 1-inch cubes
1½ cups thinly sliced onions
½ cup water
1/4 teaspoon pepper
1 pound fresh mushrooms, sliced

1/4 cup lemon juice
5-ounce can water chestnuts, sliced and drained
10-ounce package frozen Italian green beans
1½ cups cooked rice

Melt butter in a large skillet over moderate heat. Add lamb cubes and cook until browned on all sides. Add onion and cook until tender. Add water and simmer, covered, over moderately low heat for about 30 minutes. Add salt, pepper, mushrooms, lemon juice, chestnuts, and green beans and stir to blend well. Cover and simmer 10 minutes longer. Serve over rice.

Serves 4

*T*he green onions lend an unusual flavor to the lamb, as does the texture and taste of Risotto & Mushrooms (p. 82), served with a Curried Broccoli & Cauliflower Salad (p. 149). I prefer a chilled rosé wine with this supper dish.

Lamb with Green Onions

1	pound boneless lamb	2	tablespoons cooking oil
2	tablespoons soy sauce	2	cloves garlic, minced
1	tablespoon dry sherry	8	green onions, bias-sliced into
1/2	teaspoon pepper		1 1/2-inch lengths

Partially freeze lamb; slice thin, into bite-size strips. In small bowl combine the soy sauce, dry sherry, and pepper. Set aside. Preheat a large skillet over high heat; add cooking oil. Cook garlic in oil 30 seconds. Add meat; quickly cook meat, stir-fry fashion, for 3 minutes. Add green onions and soy mixture; cook for an additional 2 minutes or until onions are crisp-tender. Serve at once.

Serves 4

*D*ip a hot, buttered piece of French bread into the pan juices of this hearty dish, and wash it down with a glass of Cabernet Sauvignon.

Vegetable & Lamb Chop Skillet

4	lamb rib chops *or* loin chops	2	small zucchini, cut into 1/2-inch
1	tablespoon olive oil		pieces
1/4	teaspoon dried marjoram, crushed	2	small onions, sliced
1/2	teaspoon pepper	1	medium green pepper, cut into
1	clove garlic, minced		strips
1/2	cup water	1/4	teaspoon salt
1	chicken bouillon cube	1/4	teaspoon white pepper
8	small new potatoes (peel center strip)	2	medium tomatoes, cut into wedges
		1	tablespoon snipped parsley

Brown lamb chops in hot oil in a 12-inch skillet. Drain excess fat. Sprinkle meat with marjoram and pepper. Add garlic. Stir in water and bouillon cube. Bring to a boil; reduce heat. Simmer, covered, 10 minutes. Arrange potatoes around chops. Simmer, covered, 20 minutes more or till potatoes are almost tender. Add the zucchini, onions, green pepper, salt, and pepper. Simmer 10 minutes more, or until zucchini and green pepper are tender. Add the tomato wedges and cook, covered, 3 minutes or till heated through. Sprinkle with snipped parsley. Serve from skillet with pan juices spooned over each serving.

Serves 4

Pasta
The Basics

P asta comes in as many shapes and sizes as the imagination can picture: long and narrow, solid and hollow, flat and tube-shaped, or short and broad.

They are all fun to cook with, and the following is a descriptive listing of the different kinds of pasta, their cooking names, and cooking times.

Why limit your Italian dinners to spaghetti and meatballs when you have so much to choose from? An added plus when cooking with pasta, it goes so well with other food flavors.

"Ticker tape ain't spaghetti."

Fiorello H. LaGuardia

Kinds of Pasta	Cooking Times
Acini di pepe (peppercorn shaped pasta for soups)	5 to 6 minutes
Anelli (rings, for soups)	9 to 10 minutes
Bucatini (a long, hollow pasta, thinner than spaghetti)	9 to 10 minutes
Capellini ("angel hair," a long, delicate pasta)	8 minutes
Cavatelli (short, curled noodle)	12 minutes
Conchiglie (medium shells)	15 minutes
Conchigliette (small shells)	8 to 9 minutes
Conchiglione (jumbo shells)	23 to 25 minutes
Ditali (thimbles)	12 to 14 minutes
Ditalini (small thimbles for soup)	8 to 9 minutes
Elbow macaroni (semi-circular, hollow pasta)	10 minutes
Farfalle (butterflies)	10 minutes
Fettuccine (ribbons, straight or curled)	10 to 12 minutes
Fusilli (twists)	15 minutes
Lasagne (broad, flat macaroni)	10 to 12 minutes
Linguine (a long, flat noodle)	8 to 10 minutes
Mafalda (long, ridged noodles)	12 to 14 minutes
Manicotti (sleeves)	18 minutes
Mostaccioli (small quills)	14 minutes
Rigatoni (fat, ridged-tubed pasta)	15 minutes
Spaghetti (a long, thin pasta)	10 to 12 minutes
Tripolini (little bows for soup)	5 to 6 minutes
Vermicelli (thinner than spaghetti)	5 to 6 minutes
Ziti (hollow pasta cut short)	14 minutes

Perfect Pasta

3	quarts boiling water	1	tablespoon vegetable *or* olive oil
1	tablespoon salt	8	ounces pasta

In a large saucepan, bring the 3 quarts of water to a rapid boil. Add the salt and oil. Gradually add the pasta (don't break up spaghetti or other forms of long pasta—it will settle into the water as it becomes pliable). Be sure the water continues to boil rapidly. Stir occasionally with a wooden spoon to keep the pasta moving and prevent sticking. After 6 minutes of rapid boiling, taste for doneness. It generally takes from 8 to 10 minutes for pasta to reach the *al dente* stage, when it will taste tender, but still firm.

Overcooked pasta is mushy and far less flavorful than the *al dente* (to the tooth) method. Pasta that is to receive further cooking in a casserole should be boiled a shorter time.

Immediately drain the pasta in a colander. Serve as quickly as possible, or mix with other ingredients in the recipe, for freshly cooked pasta is the very best kind there is. *Do not rinse* unless the pasta is to be used in a cold salad. Then, rinse with cold water and drain again.

Makes about 4 cups cooked pasta

T his creamy light pasta dish can be accompanied by a simple salad of sliced tomatoes, chopped green onions, and mushrooms with Italian dressing, bread sticks, and a chilled bottle of rosé.

Asparagus & Pasta

1	pound fresh asparagus bias-sliced into 1-inch pieces	2	tablespoons butter *or* margarine
½	cup chopped onion	¾	cup light cream
½	cup chopped celery	⅛	teaspoon ground nutmeg
4	ounces fully cooked ham *or* prosciutto (about ¾ cup)		Salt and pepper
		⅓	cup grated Parmesan cheese
		10	ounces hot cooked spaghetti

In small amount of boiling salted water, cook asparagus in covered saucepan for 8 to 10 minutes. Drain. In a large saucepan, cook onion, celery, and ham or prosciutto in butter or margarine for 5 minutes or until vegetables are tender. Add cream, nutmeg, a pinch of salt, and black pepper. Cook over medium heat about 5 minutes or till sauce is slightly thickened, stirring occasionally. Stir in cooked asparagus and heat thoroughly. Toss asparagus mixture and Parmesan cheese with pasta till coated. Serve immediately. Pass additional Parmesan cheese, if desired.

Serves 4

T *he Bolognese meat sauce or ragu is one of my particular favorites. Maybe it's because, whenever I make it, I can still recall the air of romance floating around me in that tiny Italian restaurant in Easthampton summers ago.*

Conchiglie Bolognese

3 slices finely chopped uncooked bacon
1 pound ground beef
½ pound veal *or* pork *or* beef
   28-ounce can tomatoes, cut up
   Optional: 2 or 3 chicken livers, chopped
1 cup chopped onion
¼ cup of each of following:
   Carrot, chopped
   Celery, chopped
   Parsley, snipped

   salt and pepper
½ cup dry white wine
¼ cup water
   Tomato paste, about 2 tablespoons
½ teaspoon instant chicken bouillon granules
⅛ teaspoon ground nutmeg
   Optional: ⅓ cup light cream or milk
10 ounces cooked conchiglie (medium-size shells)
   Parmesan cheese

In a Dutch oven, or large saucepan, cook bacon until crisp. Add ground meat and cook until browned. Drain off fat. Add undrained tomatoes, chicken livers, onion, carrot, celery, parsley, salt, and pepper to meat mixture. Stir in wine and ¼ cup water. Bring to boil, reduce heat. Add tomato paste, bouillon, and nutmeg. Boil gently, uncovered, for 45 to 60 minutes. Just before serving, you may wish to stir cream or milk into hot sauce. Serve with pasta and Parmesan cheese.

Serves 4

*I*f you're serving this recipe as a side dish, try a different twist; couple it with Chicken Veronique (p. 26) and a spicy Italian salad with mixed romaine and iceberg lettuce, marinated artichoke hearts, and sweet red pepper cut in strips, topped with a creamy garlic dressing.

Fusilli with Broccoli

⅓ cup chopped onion	¾ cup water
¾ cup shredded carrot	Pinch pepper
1 tablespoon butter *or* margarine	12 ounces fusilli (twists)
8 medium-size mushrooms, sliced	1½ cups fresh broccoli
10½-ounce can condensed cream of chicken soup	Grated Parmesan cheese

In a 10-inch skillet, cook onion and carrot in butter or margarine over medium heat for 3 minutes or till vegetables are tender. Stir in mushrooms, soup, water and pepper. Bring to a boil. Stir in fusilli pasta. Return to a boil. Reduce heat, cover and simmer for about 10 minutes. Add broccoli. Cook 8 minutes more or until broccoli and noodles are tender, stirring occasionally. Remove mixture to serving platter. Sprinkle cheese on top.

Makes 8-side dish servings or 4 entree servings

*A*s a delightful entree to this side dish, you might serve Sautéed Scallops and Shrimp in White Wine (p. 108), or Filet of Sole Amandine (p. 86). Either of the two make a memorable combination with the fettucini. For a light salad, serve Asparagus Vinaigrette (p. 140).

Pasta with Butter and Cream

2 tablespoons butter *or* margarine	8 ounces hot cooked pasta (fettuccine)
⅔ cup grated Parmesan cheese	Fresh ground black pepper
¼ cup snipped parsley	Optional: ground nutmeg
¼ cup whipping cream *or* light cream	

In a small saucepan, melt butter or margarine. Stir in Parmesan cheese, parsley, and cream. Toss cheese mixture with pasta till coated. Season to taste with pepper; sprinkle with nutmeg, if so desired. Serve immediately. Pass additional Parmesan cheese.

Serves 4 as a side dish

I *f there is any pasta left over, just chill it overnight, refresh it with some more fresh vegetables, and serve it up as a late-night snack.*

Pasta Primavera

½ pound broccoli	1 teaspoon dried basil, crushed
1 cup sliced cauliflowerets	½ teaspoon salt
1 medium zucchini, bias-sliced	Pinch of pepper
2 large tomatoes, chopped coarsely	½ cup Gruyère cheese, shredded
½ cup chopped onion	⅓ cup snipped parsley
1 tablespoon butter	12 ounces cooked ziti
1 cup light cream	Parmesan cheese

Cut off broccoli buds, set aside. Cut stalks crosswise into ½-inch thick slices. In large covered saucepan, cook broccoli stalks and cauliflowerets in a small amount of boiling water for 5 minutes. Add broccoli buds, tomatoes, and squash, return to boiling. Reduce heat and cook about 5 minutes longer, or until vegetables are tender. Drain. Meanwhile, in a medium saucepan, cook onion in one tablespoon butter till tender, but not brown. Stir in cream, basil, ½ teaspoon salt, and a pinch of pepper. Boil gently (uncovered) about 4 minutes or till mixture is slightly thickened, stirring occasionally. Stir about ½ cup of mixture into Gruyère. Return to remaining hot mixture, heat just till cheese is melted. Stir in parsley and cooked vegetables. Pour vegetable sauce over pasta; toss till coated. Serve with grated Parmesan cheese.

Serves 4

T o further enhance this entree, try rimming each linguine-filled bowl with steamed clams still in the shell. A unique presentation, served with hot Italian bread for dipping in the sauce, and chilled glasses of soave.

Linguine with White Clam Sauce

⅓   cup olive or vegetable oil
2   cloves garlic, minced
¼   cup green onions, thinly sliced
2   7½-ounce cans minced or chopped clams, undrained, or 1 quart clams, shucked with juice
¼   cup dry white wine

Generous sprinkling Italian seasoning
1   pound cooked linguine
Optional: fresh parsley, Parmesan cheese, pinch red pepper

Heat oil in a large skillet over moderate heat. Add garlic and onions and cook for 5 minutes. Remove garlic. Add clams with juice and white wine, and season with the Italian seasoning, salt and pepper, and a pinch of red pepper if desired. Cover and simmer over low heat for 5 minutes. Toss together with cooked linguine and garnish with parsley and lots of Parmesan cheese, if desired.

Serves 6

A sparagus Vinaigrette (p. 140) on romaine lettuce with sesame breadsticks and a bottle of full-bodied Chianti complement this perfectly.

Pasta with Green Onions and Vermouth

6   sweet or hot Italian sausages or combination of both
3   tablespoons olive oil
2   cups sliced mushrooms
    16-ounce can tomato sauce
6   green onions

1   clove garlic
1   cup Italian dry vermouth
    Freshly ground pepper
½   cup Parmesan cheese
12   ounces spaghetti, cooked and drained

In a large skillet, parboil the sausages until they lose their reddish color. Throw off the water, and adding one tablespoon olive oil, brown the sausages on all sides. Remove sausages from skillet, slice as thinly as possible, and set aside.

Scrape the sausage particles in the pan together, and add two tablespoons of olive oil. Cook the mushrooms till lightly browned, then return the sausages to the skillet, adding the tomato sauce to the mixture. Stir all ingredients and cook on low heat for 35 to 45 minutes. Wash the green onions, and split each one down the center, then slice horizontally in three. In another pan, cook the garlic in olive oil together with the green onions till pale in color. Add the vermouth and black pepper to the sauce and stir. Place the green onions on top of the pasta with sauce to cover. Serve with Parmesan cheese.

Serves 4

W hether you decide to serve this tuna dish hot or chilled, an appetizing accompaniment is broccoli flowerets vinaigrette, topped with hard-boiled eggs cut in eighths.

Tuna Noodlelini

2   10½-ounce cans cream of
      mushroom soup
2   medium onions chopped
¾   tablespoon butter *or* margarine
3   7-ounce cans of white meat
      (albacore) tuna in water, drained
1   pound cooked conchiglie (medium
      shells)

      8-ounce can baby peas, heated
2   teaspoons Italian seasoning
1   teaspoon garlic salt
      Seasoned bread crumbs
      Parmesan cheese

Cook soup according to package instructions. Lightly brown onions in butter or margarine. Add the tuna and cooked onions to the soup mixture. Cook the shells until just tender and drain. *Do not rinse.* Pour the hot soup mixture over the shells and blend well. Add the heated peas, Italian seasoning, and garlic salt and blend again. Turn mixture into a serving dish, and sprinkle the top with a touch of seasoned bread crumbs and Parmesan cheese. Serve with additional Parmesan cheese, if so desired.

Serves 4 to 6

M y mother, although she didn't realize it, taught me to cook, and this was the very first recipe I prepared on my own in her kitchen. She was delighted and surprised to find that I could be interested in something other than playing ball with my brothers.

Rigatoni & Meatballs in Meat Sauce

Meat Sauce

1 pound ground beef	1 cup Burgundy
1 large onion, chopped	28-ounce can tomatoes, undrained and cut up
2 cloves garlic, minced	16-ounce can tomato sauce
2 teaspoons Italian seasoning	

Brown meat, and add lightly cooked onions and garlic, with Italian seasoning, wine, tomatoes, and tomato sauce. Simmer over low heat for 45 minutes before adding cooked meatballs.

Meatballs

2 cups seasoned bread crumbs	½ teaspoon dried oregano leaves, crushed
2 eggs slightly beaten	
1 pound ground beef	1 teaspoon salt
¼ cup grated Parmesan cheese	3 tablespoons butter or margarine
2 tablespoons dried parsley flakes, crushed	1 pound rigatoni

Mix together bread crumbs, eggs, beef, cheese, parsley, oregano, and salt. Shape into 20 small balls. Melt butter in skillet over moderate heat, brown meatballs on all sides. Remove from heat. Ten minutes before serving time, heat meat sauce and meatballs over low heat until piping hot, stirring frequently.

Cook rigatoni for 15 minutes and drain. Serve sauce and meatballs over rigatoni.

Serves 4 to 6

"Cooking is like love. It should be entered into with abandon or not at all."

Harriet Van Horne

I *just made this dish the other night for some visiting friends. We began the meal with a salad of chilled, crunchy iceberg lettuce, sliced mushrooms, and marinated artichoke hearts, topped with a creamy garlic dressing. We ate all the salad, drank all the wine (Valpolicella), and cleaned our dinner plates with hot French bread.*

Mostaccioli with Sausages

1	pound sweet Italian sausage	2	8-ounce cans tomato sauce
1	tablespoon olive oil		Pinch sugar
2	medium red *or* green peppers	1	teaspoon dried marjoram, crushed
1	cup chopped onion		Salt and pepper
1	clove garlic, minced	12	ounces hot cooked mostaccioli
	28-ounce can tomatoes, finely cut	½	cup grated Parmesan cheese

In a large skillet, parboil the sausages until they lose their red color. Drain well. In 1 tablespoon olive oil, cook sausages until browned on all sides. If necessary, add a little more oil, and red or green pepper, onion, and garlic, and cook till vegetables are tender. Stir in cut tomatoes, tomato sauce, sugar, marjoram, salt, and pepper. Bring to a boil, then reduce heat and cover and cook for 45 minutes. Spoon off any fat. Place cooked pasta on platter, and spoon over the sauce. Serve with grated Parmesan cheese.

Serves 4

T *his dish makes a great late-night snack, or you may serve it as the first course, to be followed with Easy-Does-It Chicken (p. 25) or Poached Halibut in Clam Sauce (p. 90), and a tossed green salad with a creamy Italian dressing.*

Spaghetti with Garlic & Olive Oil

2	cloves garlic, minced	⅛	teaspoon red pepper flakes
3	tablespoons olive oil		Freshly ground black pepper
¼	cup snipped parsley	8	ounces cooked spaghetti
¼	teaspoon salt		Parmesan cheese

In a small skillet, cook garlic in olive oil till golden brown. Stir in parsley, salt, red pepper flakes, and black pepper. Heat and stir for 3 minutes. Toss garlic mixture with spaghetti till coated. Serve immediately with Parmesan cheese.

Serves 4 as a side dish

T *his is a "rave" side dish when accompanied by Osso Buco (p. 134) or Filet of Sole Amandine (p. 86) and a pretty platter filled with Broccoli with Lemon Sauce (p. 142). For the wine, only a Johannisburg Riesling will do.*

Vermicelli with Mushrooms and Prosciutto

3	cups sliced fresh mushrooms	1	teaspoon dried basil, crushed
½	medium green pepper, cut in strips	½	teaspoon pepper
¼	cup butter *or* margarine	10	ounces hot cooked vermicelli
2	ounces prosciutto (Italian ham)		Parmesan cheese
¼	cup snipped parsley		

In a saucepan, cook mushrooms and green pepper in butter or margarine over medium heat about 5 minutes or until tender. Add prosciutto cut into strips, parsley, dried basil, and pepper to taste. Toss mushroom mixture with hot cooked pasta. Serve immediately with Parmesan cheese.

Serves 4 as a side dish

W *hen I was a little kid, sometimes after Sunday Mass one of my best-friend classmates would invite me over to have an early Italian supper with her family. I remember her mother served four or five main dishes with lots of salad and red wine. This was one of those dishes.*

Ziti with Italian Sausage

1	pound Italian sweet *or* hot sausages *or* combination of both	1	teaspoon salt
		⅛	teaspoon pepper
3	medium-size onions, chopped	½	teaspoon oregano
½	pound mushrooms, sliced	½	teaspoon dried basil, crushed
4	cups canned tomatoes, undrained and chopped	12	ounces ziti
			Parmesan cheese, grated

Parboil sausages in small amount of water, then drain water and cook the sausage in a large skillet until browned. Remove and set aside. Add onions; cook until tender. Add mushrooms to onions and cook till vegetables are golden brown. Add sausage, tomatoes, salt and pepper, oregano, and basil. Cook uncovered over moderately low heat for 30 to 40 minutes, until slightly thickened. Spoon sausage and sauce over cooked ziti, and sprinkle with grated Parmesan cheese.

Serves 4

Pasta Salads

T his salad is perfect for a seaside picnic.

By the Sea-Shell Salad

1 pound medium- or small-size shrimp, cooked, peeled, and deveined
12 ounces conchigliette (small shells)
½ cup chopped celery
½ cup radishes, thinly sliced
⅓ cup chopped green pepper
¾ cup tomato, diced
⅓ cup green onion, chopped
1 cup mayonnaise
½ cup Italian salad dressing
½ cup chili sauce
Salt and freshly ground pepper to taste

Cook shrimp till pink in color. Cool, peel, and devein. Rinse with cold water. Cook pasta shells 8 minutes or till just tender. Rinse in cold water, and drain well. Combine shrimp with pasta and celery, radishes, green pepper, tomato, and onion. Mix well. Combine mayonnaise, Italian dressing, and chili sauce together, blend well with salt and pepper. Fold into shrimp and pasta mixture, and chill for 2 to 3 hours. Arrange on mixed salad greens, if desired.

Serves 6 to 8

"Gather a shell from the strown beach
And listen at its lips: they sigh
The same desire and mystery,
The echo of the whole sea's speech."

D. G. Rosetti

T his is an easy salad to prepare and is very portable.

Green and White Pasta Salad

10 ounces medium pasta shells (conchiglie)
¾ pound broccoli
1 egg
½ cup olive oil
4 anchovies
2 cloves garlic
2 tablespoons lemon juice

2 7-ounce cans albacore (white) tuna in water, drained
1 cup pitted ripe olives, whole *or* halves
1 green pepper, cut into strips
½ cup grated Parmesan cheese

Cook shells in salted boiling water until *al dente*. Rinse in cold water and drain well. Wash and peel broccoli stems and slice diagonally, ½-inch thick. Snip flowerets from stems, and steam all until crisp-tender (bright green). Drain and cool under cold water. Break egg into blender. With motor running, slowly add olive oil. Add anchovies, garlic, and lemon juice, and process until smooth. In large bowl, toss dressing with warm shells, broccoli, tuna, olives, green pepper, and Parmesan cheese. Serve at room temperature in lettuce-lined bowl.

Serves 4

A s a delightful appetizer to this main dish, try the Clams & White Wine Broth (p. 94) with plenty of garlic bread for dipping, and a cold bottle of rosé Anjou for sipping.

Fettuccine Salad

2 medium tomatoes
2 medium cucumbers
¾ cup mayonnaise
¾ cup sour cream
3 tablespoons tarragon vinegar *or* other herb vinegar

2½ tablespoons chopped fresh dill
2 tablespoons grated onion
12 ounces fettuccine
Salt and freshly ground pepper to taste

Core tomatoes and plunge into boiling water for 1 minute. Transfer to a bowl of cold water, and peel the skins. Halve the tomatoes and squeeze out the seeds and juice. Dice into small pieces. Peel cucumbers, cut in half lengthwise, scoop out seeds, and dice into ¼-inch pieces (about 1¾ cups) Reserve. In a large mixing bowl, combine mayonnaise, sour cream, vinegar, dill, and grated onion. Mix well. Add diced tomato and cucumber. In a large pot of boiling, salted water, cook fettuccine for 10 minutes or until just tender. Drain, rinse, and submerge in ice water until cooled. Drain thoroughly. Add pasta to the bowl of dressing, and toss well. Season with salt, pepper, and additional vinegar, to taste.

Serves 4 as a main dish

> "A cucumber should be well-sliced and dressed with pepper and vinegar, and then thrown out as good for nothing."
>
> Samuel Johnson

A delightful side dish for dining al fresco, when accompanied by a platter of various cheeses, plenty of French bread and assorted crackers, waiting to be washed down by a fruity white Burgundy cooler.

Italian Sausage Salad

6	Italian-style sausages, sweet *or* hot	¼	cup olive oil
1	teaspoon cooking oil	3	tablespoons wine vinegar
8	ounces fusilli (twists)	1	clove garlic, chopped
3	green peppers, peeled and seeded, cut into strips	½	teaspoon garlic salt
2	red onions, thinly sliced		Freshly ground black pepper to taste
1	8-ounce can of kidney beans		Pinch oregano
3	hard-cooked eggs, quartered		
3	tablespoons chopped parsley		

To cook the sausages, put them in a skillet with water to cover; parboil to heat, then reduce heat and poach for one minute. Drain water; slice the sausage into ½-inch lengths, and fry over medium heat in an oiled skillet until nicely browned. Cook and rinse the pasta, then drain well. Combine the sausage, peppers, onions, pasta, kidney beans, eggs, and parsley in a bowl. In a second bowl, combine the olive oil, vinegar, garlic, salt, pepper, and oregano. Beat vigorously with a fork and pour the dressing over the salad, tossing gently. Place salad in the refrigerator for a few hours to chill. Serve on red-leaf lettuce.

Serves 6

T *he only thing this exquisite salad needs is to be eaten.*

Pasta Primavera Salad

12 ounces fettuccine verde or spinach linguine

⅔ cup carrots, cut in half lengthwise, then thinly sliced

1 cup broccoli flowerets

⅔ cup zucchini, cut in half lengthwise, then thinly sliced

½ cup green pepper, diced

Salad Dressing

⅔ cup sour cream

¾ cup mayonnaise

½ teaspoon Worcestershire sauce

2 tablespoons tarragon vinegar

1 small clove garlic, minced

2 tablespoons thinly sliced green onions

2 tablespoons chopped parsley

Salt and freshly ground pepper to taste

In a large pot, place pasta in boiling, salted water, and cook 8 to 10 minutes, or until just tender. Drain, chill rapidly in cold water, and drain thoroughly. Blanch carrots and broccoli in 2 cups boiling, salted water for 1 minute. Chill rapidly in cold water and drain thoroughly.

Combine dressing ingredients in a large bowl and blend together. Add pasta and vegetables, and toss well. Sprinkle salt and pepper to taste and serve.

Serves 4 as a main dish

"The discovery of a new dish does more for the happiness of man than the discovery of a new star."

Brillat-Savarin

S erve pita bread with this curry salad and watch who gets stuffed first.

Pasta Chicken-Curry Salad

½ cup golden raisins	Salt
1 cup chopped apples	¾ teaspoon curry powder
½ cup chicken broth	¼ teaspoon garlic salt
3 cups julienne-cut (strips) cooked chicken	¼ teaspoon black pepper
	¾ cup mayonnaise
¼ cup chopped red onion	Salted peanuts
10 ounces cooked elbow macaroni	Chopped parsley
2 tablespoons fresh ginger	

Combine raisins and apples with chicken broth in a saucepan and let stand five minutes. Add chicken and onion and heat to serving temperature. Mix hot chicken mixture with hot macaroni. Stir in ginger, salt, curry powder, garlic salt, pepper, and mayonnaise. Blend and chill well. Serve with peanuts and parsley.

Serves 6 to 8

"Diet: Something to take the starch out of you."

Anonymous

I love options in recipes, don't you? It gives you so much more to think about.

Pasta Summer Supper Salad

12 ounces cooked spaghettini broken into 4-inch lengths	2 teaspoons salt
¼ cup lemon juice	½ teaspoon coarse black pepper
2 tablespoons oil	½ cup sour cream
1 cup sliced celery	½ cup mayonnaise
½ cup chopped green onions	3 tablespoons wine vinegar
1 cup blanched zucchini slices	Optional: Julienne strips of turkey, ham, and cheese
16 cherry tomatoes, halved	Lettuce

Drain and rinse cooked pasta in cold water. Rinse thoroughly. Place in bowl, stir in lemon juice and oil, and chill for at least one hour. Add celery, onion, zucchini, tomatoes, salt, pepper, sour cream, mayonnaise, and wine vinegar. Mix thoroughly. Add meat and cheese if desired. Chill well. Line salad bowl with lettuce, and spoon salad on lettuce leaves.

Serves 8

A longside this unusual sesame salad, serve a platter of Lamb with Green
Onions (p. 45).

Sesame Pasta Salad

12 ounces linguine
1/4 cup red pepper, diced small

1/4 cup green onion, thinly sliced

Salad Dressing

1/4 cup white wine vinegar
1/3 cup canned chicken broth
1/4 cup sesame oil
1/2 cup soy sauce
2 tablespoons sugar

1 tablespoon ginger, peeled and finely
     chopped
4 drops hot sauce
3/4 cup creamy peanut butter
     Sesame seeds

Place linguine in a large pot of salted, boiling water. Cook 8 minutes, till almost tender. Chill rapidly in cool water and drain thoroughly. Mix all dressing
ingredients, except sesame seeds, and blend well. Toss pasta with peppers,
green onions, and dressing. Sprinkle with sesame seeds.

Serves 4 as a main dish

I can't think of anything better than crab salad, except maybe starting with a
huge bowl of Lulu Brown's Boiled Shrimp (p. 109).

Vermicelli Crab Salad

1 tablespoon horseradish
1 cup chili sauce
2 tablespoons lemon juice
2 tablespoons chopped green onion
1 small clove garlic, crushed
1/8 teaspoon dried dill

1/2 cup rosé wine
1 pound fresh *or* canned crabmeat
10 ounces vermicelli (thin noodles)
     Romaine and iceberg lettuce, mixed
3 hard-cooked eggs, quartered
     Optional: ripe olives

Combine horseradish, chili sauce, lemon juice, onion, garlic, dill, and wine.
Add half of crabmeat to sauce and chill thoroughly for several hours. Cook
pasta till tender in boiling salted water. Rinse in cold water and drain well. Toss
with crab meat mixture. Chill well. Arrange greens on serving plates, and
top with crab salad mixture. Arrange remaining crab meat over salad, and garnish with egg quarters and olives. Serve very cold.

Serves 6 to 8

S *alads always make me think of hot summer days, so let's sit on the patio* *with a pitcher or two of cranberry cooler, toss the tortellini around, and have a* *really good time.*

Tortellini Salad

12	ounces cheese tortellini	3	tomatoes, cut into eighths
1	cup broccoli flowerets		Salt and pepper
½	cup mushroom caps, quartered		

Salad Dressing

¼	cup red wine vinegar	¼	teaspoon garlic, minced
1	teaspoon dried oregano leaves	½	teaspoon salt
1½	teaspoons Dijon mustard	⅛	teaspoon pepper
1	teaspoon dried marjoram leaves	½	cup olive oil *or* vegetable oil
½	teaspoon dried thyme leaves		

In a large pot, place the tortellini in boiling, salted water, and cook for 6 to 7 minutes, or till just tender. Chill rapidly in cool water, and drain thoroughly.

Blanch broccoli in boiling, salted water for 1 minute. Chill rapidly in cold water, and drain thoroughly. Wash mushrooms and pat dry.

Mix dressing ingredients (excluding oil). Vigorously whisk in oil. Toss tortellini together with broccoli, mushrooms, and tomatoes. Fold in dressing. Add salt and pepper to taste.

Serves 4 as a main dish

"Treat your friends as you do your pictures, *And put them in their best light."*

Jennie Jerome Churchill

W *hat's a macaroni salad without a platter full of Finger-Lickin' Fried Chicken & Gravy (p. 26) and lots of ice-cold watermelon?*

Willy-Dilly Macaroni Salad

10 ounces elbow macaroni	¼ cup chopped celery
1 cup American cheese, cubed	¼ cup chopped green pepper
16-ounce can (2 cups) cut green beans, drained	4 tablespoons chopped pimiento
15½-ounce can (2 cups) red kidney beans	¾ cup salad dressing *or* mayonnaise
	1 tablespoon wine vinegar
1 small onion, thinly sliced	1 teaspoon salt
	¾ teaspoon dill weed

Cook macaroni until barely tender. Rinse, drain well, and cool. Combine macaroni with American cheese cubes, cut green beans, kidney beans, onion, celery, green pepper, and pimiento. Blend together salad dressing or mayonnaise, vinegar, salt, and dill weed. Add to macaroni mixture. Toss lightly. Cover and chill well. Serve salad in lettuce-lined bowl.

Serves 6

*"I cast my net in many streams
To catch the silverfish of dreams."*

Karle Wilson Baker

Pork
The Basics

Pork demands thorough cooking. No matter what cut of pork your recipe calls for, all fresh pork should be well done.

For cooking off the top of your stove, pork chops and pork steaks are best suited for braising, as they tend to become dry when broiled.

Pork tenderloins, because they are small (about three-fourths of a pound to a pound each), also do well prepared on the stove top. The pork tenderloin is a long and tender piece of pork and is sold whole. Depending on the recipe, you can then cut it into thick slices or flatten it into cutlets.

Fresh spareribs are meaty and pink in color and are sold by the sheet, or side. If you cook them by the sheet, ask your butcher to crack through the ribs at the large end so they'll be less difficult to cut into serving portions.

*A*s kids in New York, we used to love to go swimming in this pool down on Avenue A; after spending the whole day there, we'd built up quite an appetite. On the street corner, there was an old man selling these sausage "heros," and my brother and I, with hair still dripping wet, would eat and laugh ourselves all the way home.

Hot & Sweet Italian Sausage "Heros" with Green Peppers & Onions

12 Italian sausages (6 hot and 6 sweet)
4 large green peppers, seeded and cut into strips
3 large onions, in round slices
1/2 cup olive oil
6 hero rolls

Prick sausages with a fork. Parboil sausages in a large skillet for 10 minutes. Drain and remove. Add a portion of the olive oil to the skillet, add sausages, and cook slowly over moderate heat, until well-browned on all sides. Remove sausages from the skillet and keep warm. Add the remainder of the olive oil, and place the peppers and onions in the skillet to cook until tender and browned. Place two sausages on each roll, and heap with peppers and onions.

Serves 6

"Man is the only animal that eats when he is not hungry, drinks when he is not thirsty, and makes love at all seasons."

Anonymous

*A*dd Parsley New Potatoes (p. 156), a lettuce-leaf platter of Chilled Herbed Mushrooms (p. 146), and hot dinner rolls to round out the dinner menu.

Braised Tenderloin & Snow Peas

1/2 cup finely chopped onion
3 tablespoons vegetable oil
3/4 pound whole pork tenderloin
1/2 cup dry white wine
2 8-ounce packages frozen snow pea pods, slightly thawed
1/4 cup water

In a large pre-heated skillet, cook onion in vegetable oil, until tender. Remove onion and set aside. Cut tenderloin into 1-inch diagonal slices and flatten slightly with a mallet. Cook meat in skillet over moderately high heat until lightly browned on both sides. Add reserved onion and wine; cover and simmer 30 minutes over low heat. Remove meat. Add peas and water to skillet; mix well. Place meat over vegetables. Cover and simmer 3 to 4 minutes, until peas are just tender. Arrange meat slices on a serving platter and spoon vegetables around the meat.

Serves 4

"How luscious lies the pea within the pod."

Emily Dickinson

*A*n ideal vegetable to serve with this Oriental pork recipe is the Asparagus & Tomato Toss (p. 140). For dessert, orange sherbet topped with mandarin orange slices and slivered almonds.

Peking Pork Chops & Rice

1½ pounds pork steaks, cut ½-inch thick
1 tablespoon peanut or vegetable oil
 8-ounce can crushed pineapple
2 tablespoons soy sauce
2 tablespoons white vinegar
1 teaspoon sugar

½ teaspoon ground ginger
1 teaspoon cayenne pepper
1 small onion, cut into wedges
1 small green pepper, cut into strips
 8-ounce can sliced water chestnuts
1½ teaspoons cornstarch
2 cups cooked long-grain rice

Cut steaks into bite-size pieces. In a large skillet, quickly brown meat in hot oil on all sides. Remove from skillet and set aside. Drain crushed pineapple, reserving juice; add enough water to juice to make ½ cup liquid. Combine juice mixture with soy sauce, vinegar, sugar, ground ginger, and cayenne. Add mixture and onion wedges to skillet, return the browned meat to the skillet, and cook till tender over low heat for about 20 minutes. Add green pepper strips and water chestnuts; cover and simmer for about 3 minutes. Combine the crushed pineapple and cornstarch, and add to skillet. Cook and stir till mixture is thickened and bubbly. Cook and stir 1 to 2 minutes more. Spoon mixture over hot cooked rice.

Serves 4

*"Life to have its sweets must have its sours.
Love isn't always two souls picking flowers."*

John Masefield

I like doubling this recipe and serving it at an informal get-together during the football season, when the tennis championships are played, or whenever good friends with a common interest want to celebrate life.

Knockout Knockwurst Skillet

1	medium onion, sliced	1	cup dry white wine
2	cloves garlic, minced	1	teaspoon caraway seed
2	tablespoons butter *or* margarine		8-ounce can applesauce
2	medium potatoes, peeled and sliced		16-ounce jar sauerkraut
1	cup water	1	pound knockwurst (about 4)
1	beef bouillon cube		

In a large skillet, cook onion and garlic in butter or margarine till onion is tender, but not brown. Stir in potatoes, water, bouillon cube, wine, and caraway seed. Bring to a boil; then reduce heat. Cover and simmer 10 to 15 minutes. Place applesauce, sauerkraut, and knockwurst atop the vegetable mixture, and cook until most of the liquid is absorbed; about 15 minutes.

Serves 4

> "You'll never get indigestion from swallowing your pride occasionally."
> Anonymous

A t a Chinese restaurant I once got a fortune cookie that said, "If you can't find what you want, make your own."

Fortune-Cookie Pork with Pea Pods

1	pound boneless pork	1	teaspoon grated fresh ginger
2	tablespoons soy sauce	2	cups fresh pea pods *or* 6-ounce
1	teaspoon grated orange peel		package frozen pea pods, thawed
2	teaspoons cornstarch		11-ounce can mandarin orange
½	cup orange juice		sections, drained
2	tablespoons peanut or vegetable oil		

Slice partially-frozen pork into thin bite-size strips. Blend soy sauce, orange peel, cornstarch, and orange juice together. Set aside. Preheat a large skillet over high heat; add cooking oil. Cook ginger in hot oil for 30 seconds. Add pea pods; cook 2 minutes for fresh pea pods or 1 minute for thawed frozen pea-pods. Remove pea pods, adding more oil if necessary. Add half of the pork strips to the hot skillet, for 2 to 3 minutes. Remove pork from skillet. Add remaining pork and cook 2 to 3 minutes. Placing all the pork in the skillet, stir soy sauce mixture into pork. Cook and stir until thickened and bubbly. Stir in pea pods; cover and cook 1 minute more. Remove from heat; stir in drained orange sections. Serve at once.

Serves 4

*A*n exceptional combination with the pork chops is to add Brown Rice Imperial (p. 77) and a Chilled Green Beans à la Niçoise (p. 146). The wine should not be too dry.

Pork Chops in Orange Sauce

6	loin pork chops, ¾-inch thick		1	tablespoon minced fresh parsley *or* 1 teaspoon dried parsley leaves, crushed
1	tablespoon butter *or* margarine			
1	medium onion, chopped			
1	tablespoon flour		2	tablespoons lemon juice
2	beef bouillon cubes		½	cup orange juice
1	teaspoon dry mustard		1	teaspoon salt
1	cup hot water		⅛	teaspoon pepper

Place the chops in a large preheated skillet, and cook until browned on both sides. Remove from pan and set aside. Melt the butter or margarine in the skillet, and add the onion. Cook until the onion is tender but not brown. Stir in flour; dissolve the bouillon cubes and mustard in hot water, and add slowly, stirring constantly. Cook for 5 minutes. Add parsley, lemon and orange juice, salt and pepper; blend thoroughly. Return the chops to the skillet, and cook over low heat for 25 to 35 minutes or until meat is tender.

Serves 6

*P*ersonally, I like my curry dishes to talk back to me! So, if you're like me, for an additional POW, just add another teaspoon of curry powder to this recipe.

Precious Pork Curry

3 tablespoons butter *or* margarine	½ teaspoon celery salt
1 large onion, chopped	2 chicken bouillon cubes
1 clove garlic, finely chopped	2 apples, peeled and cored and cut
1½ pounds boneless pork cut into bite-size cubes	into thin slices
½ teaspoon salt	2 cups boiling water
¼ teaspoon pepper	1 cup light cream *or* half and half
1½ tablespoons curry powder	2 tablespoons flour
	2 to 3 cups cooked long-grain rice

Melt butter or margarine in a large heavy skillet over moderate heat. Add onion and garlic and cook until soft but not browned. Add pork cubes and brown on all sides over moderately low heat. Add salt, pepper, curry powder, celery salt, chicken bouillon cubes, apples, and water. Cover tightly and cook over moderately low heat for 30 minutes or until pork is tender. Stir a little bit of the cream or half and half into the flour, and stir to form a smooth paste; add remaining cream or half and half, and blend well. Add cream to hot pork mixture; bring to a boil, stirring constantly until slightly thickened and smooth. Serve with hot cooked rice.

Serves 4 to 6

L *et's go all-the-way country with these ribs, adding a plateful of Down-Home Greens & Ham Hocks (p. 150), Bull's-Eye Black-eyes (p. 142), and a tub of Creamy Home Made Coleslaw (p. 147).*

Sherried Country-Style Pork Ribs

12 to 16 pork ribs	⅓ cup sherry
½ cup soy sauce	½ cup honey

Place the ribs in a large kettle of boiling water, and cook for 1 hour or until tender. Arrange the ribs in a large broiler pan or skillet and brown them on top of the stove. Mix the soy sauce, sherry, and honey together and stir. Pour the sherry mixture over the ribs, and cook for an additional 20 minutes.

Serves 4

W *henever I wanted to buy "greens," I'd take the A Train to 125th Street, and there on those Harlem streets, I'd find what I was looking for . . . the best greens in town. So, serve some soulful Sweet & Sour Greens (p. 161) and Bull's-Eye Black-eyes (p. 142) with rice.*

Hoot 'n' Holler Ham Steaks

Shortening	4-ounce jar chopped pimiento
4 ham steaks, cut ½- to 1-inch thick	1 clove garlic, mashed
2 tablespoons cornstarch	½ cup cider vinegar
¼ cup sugar	2 tablespoons soy sauce
¼ cup cold water	1½ tablespoons hot sauce
8-ounce can crushed pineapple	
½ cup chopped green pepper	

Rub a preheated skillet with a little shortening, add the ham slices, and cook over moderate heat, turning once, until the meat is browned. In a 1-quart saucepan, stir together the cornstarch, sugar, and water until well blended. Stir in undrained pineapple, pepper, pimiento, garlic, vinegar, soy sauce, and hot sauce. Cook over high heat for 5 minutes, stirring constantly, until clear and thickened. Let sauce stand 5 to 10 minutes to develop flavor. Pour over ham slices, and serve immediately.

Serves 4

T hese little ribs make wonderful finger-food appetizers.

Spicy Spareribs

3	cups water	1	teaspoon salt
¾	cup chopped onion	½	teaspoon pepper
½	cup soy sauce	½	teaspoon sesame oil
¼	cup dry sherry	3	pounds meaty pork spareribs,
4	slices ginger		cut in half across bones
2	teaspoons crushed aniseed	2	beaten eggs
2	cloves garlic, minced	¼	cup cornstarch
1	teaspoon sugar		Vegetable oil, for frying

In a large Dutch oven, combine water, onion, soy sauce, dry sherry, ginger, aniseed, garlic, sugar, salt, pepper, and sesame oil; mix well. Cut ribs into two sections. Add ribs to mixture in Dutch oven. Cover and simmer one hour or until tender. Drain ribs, reserving liquid. Cool ribs completely. Stir together eggs and cornstarch. Dip rib pieces in batter and coat evenly. Fry ribs a few at a time in the Dutch oven in hot oil for about 4 minutes or until golden brown. Remove ribs with a slotted spoon and drain on paper towels.

Serves 4 to 6

I n the Oriental section of most markets, you can find many varieties of wheat-flour noodles. Just cook according to package directions, adding ¼-cup sliced green onions. For the salad, drizzle a vinaigrette dressing mixed with 1 table-spoon soy sauce and 1 tablespoon of toasted sesame seeds over lightly steamed broccoli spears.

Sweet & Sour Pork

¼	cup cornstarch	½	cup chopped carrot
¼	cup flour	1	clove garlic, minced
1	beaten egg	2	tablespoons vegetable oil
	14-ounce can chicken broth	½	cup sugar
½	teaspoon salt	⅓	cup red wine vinegar
1	pound boneless pork, cut into cubes	2	teaspoons soy sauce
	Vegetable oil for frying	¼	cup cold water
1	large green pepper, seeded and	2	tablespoons cornstarch
	diced		

In a bowl, combine ¼ cup of cornstarch, flour, egg, ¼ cup of chicken broth, salt, and beat till smooth. Dip pork cubes into batter. Fry in deep skillet in hot oil for 5 to 6 minutes till golden. Drain, keep warm. In the same skillet, cook green pepper, carrot, and garlic in the 2 tablespoons oil till vegetables are tender, but not browned. Stir in remaining chicken broth, sugar, vinegar, and soy sauce. Bring to a boil; slowly blend 1/4 cup cold water into the 2 tablespoons cornstarch. Stir into vegetable mixture. Cook and stir till thickened. Stir in pork cubes.

Serves 4 to 6

I f you'd prefer to substitute something more tropical for the plain white rice, try the Bali-Hai Fried Rice (p. 76) and a spinach and bok choy salad with sliced mushrooms and a delicate honey-sesame dressing.

Hocus-Pocus Pork Chow Mein

1/3	cup soy sauce	2	cups diced cooked pork
3	tablespoons cornstarch	2	cups chopped celery
	8-ounce can sliced water chestnuts, undrained	1	medium onion, thinly sliced
1	pound fresh bean sprouts	3	cups cooked long-grain rice
1/4	pound fresh mushrooms, sliced		Chow mein noodles

In a large skillet, stir together soy sauce and cornstarch. Stir in water chestnuts, bean sprouts, and mushrooms; then add pork, celery, and onion. Cover and cook over medium heat for 20 minutes, until hot and the sauce is thickened. Stir thoroughly, and serve over cooked rice with chow mein noodles.

Serves 4

"Propaganda is baloney disguised as food for thought."

Anonymous

Rice
The Basics

Eating rice will make you wise. While that may not be an old Chinese proverb, I like to believe it's true.

Rice lends itself to the addition of innumerable seasonings and is an excellent ingredient to use in making stuffings, salads, and even desserts.

The key to making wonderful, puffy, cloud-like rice is to always use a heavy saucepan with a tight-fitting lid. Once the rice has come to a boil, don't stir it. This will only make the rice gummy. Most of all, don't peek to see how the rice is doing. If you lift the lid, the steam will escape, and the temperature will lower, causing the rice to stick.

To keep rice warm before serving, you can keep it in a covered pot for about 5 to 10 minutes, but no longer, or it will "pack."

Many ingredients can be added to rice for special taste and texture. Vegetables such as chopped onion or mushrooms will enchance the rice dish, as well as parsley, dried dill weed, pine nuts, or slivered almonds. When mixing in other ingredients, fold them in gently, and do not stir.

Cooking "Fail-Safe" Rice

1   cup long-grain white rice *or* short-grain brown rice

2   cups water or other liquid

1   tablespoon butter *or* margarine *or* vegetable oil

1   teaspoon salt

For long-grain white rice: bring the water or other liquid, and the shortening of your choice, to a rolling boil. Add salt and rice and cook in a heavy 2-quart saucepan. Reduce heat to low, and cover saucepan with a tight-fitting lid. Simmer, without lifting lid, 20 to 25 minutes, or until rice is tender.

For short-grain brown rice: add a tablespoon of oil to heated 2-quart saucepan, add 1 cup of brown rice and, stirring constantly, cook the rice for 1 minute in the hot oil. Add two cups of boiling water, reduce heat to low, and cover saucepan with a tight-fitting lid. Simmer, without lifting the lid, for 35 to 45 minutes, or until rice is tender.

If you prefer the rice to be a little moist, take the saucepan off the heat while there is a little liquid left in the pan. Let the rice rest for 5 minutes. Makes about 3 cups of cooked rice.

Serves 4

"With a handful of rice and a little dried fish, I can make a half a dozen dishes."

T. S. Eliot

F or your next deck party, either on land or at sea, marry this mouth-watering rice dish with trays of Butterfry-fly Shrimp (p. 110) and a huge bowl of Shellfish Salad (p. 104) with Bloody Marys all around.

Bali-Hai Fried Rice

2	beaten eggs	1	teaspoon grated fresh ginger
⅓	cup soy sauce	½	cup chopped green onion
2	tablespoons dry sherry	4	cups cooked rice
½	teaspoon white pepper	2	cups cooked shrimp
2	tablespoons vegetable oil	1	cup canned baby peas
1	clove garlic, minced		

In a small bowl, combine beaten eggs, soy sauce, dry sherry and pepper; set aside. In a preheated skillet, add oil, and cook garlic and ginger in hot oil for 30 seconds. Add chopped onion; cook about 1 minute or till crisp-tender. Stir in cooked rice, shrimp and peas. Cook, stirring frequently, for 6 to 8 minutes. While stirring constantly, pour egg mixture over rice, and cook, stirring constantly, until eggs are set.

Serves 4 to 6

T his rice dish may be substituted for the noodles when serving 60-Minute Stroganoff (p. 9) together with Beets & Sour Cream Salad (p. 141).

Moroccan Brown Rice

3	tablespoons vegetable oil	1½	cups sliced green pepper
1	cup short-grain brown rice	¾	cup unsalted cashew nuts
2	cups boiling water		Soy sauce
2	tablespoons butter or margarine		

In a heavy 2-quart saucepan, heat the vegetable oil over moderate flame. Add rice and stir until rice is saturated with oil. Add boiling water, reduce heat to low, and cover tightly. Simmer for 45 minutes or longer until rice is chewy. While rice is cooking, melt 2 tablespoons of butter in a skillet over moderately low heat; add green pepper and cook, stirring occasionally, until tender. Add to cooked rice. Then add cashew nuts, cover, and heat 2 minutes. Serve with soy sauce, if desired.

Serves 4

*N*ext time you're planning a picnic for the upcoming concert at the Hollywood Bowl, be sure to make this surprise dish one of your selections.

Bonanza Brown Rice Salad

2 cups cubed, cooked chicken
3 cups cooked brown rice
1/2 cup sliced celery
1/2 cup chopped apple
1/4 cup sliced green onion

1/2 cup mayonnaise *or* salad dressing
1/4 cup Italian salad dressing
1/2 cup chopped walnuts
Lettuce

In a mixing bowl, combine chicken, cooked brown rice, celery, apple, and
green onion. Stir together mayonnaise or salad dressing with Italian salad
dressing and pour into chicken mixture. Toss gently to coat. Cover and chill.
Just before serving, add walnuts and toss again. Serve in individual lettuce-
lined salad bowls.

Serves 4 to 5

*T*his royal rice recipe is so regal, it should only be served on purple-encrusted
plates bearing the motto: "Long Live the Cook!"

Brown Rice Imperial

1/4 cup vegetable oil
2 cups short-grain brown rice
1 teaspoon salt
3 tablespoons soy sauce
3 cubes beef bouillon
4 cups of boiling water
   7-ounce can sliced water chestnuts,
      drained

1 bunch green onions, chopped
1/4 pound fresh mushrooms, sliced
1 cup slivered almonds
1 teaspoon salt
1 tablespoon white pepper

Pour the vegetable oil into a heavy 2-quart saucepan, and heat over moderate
flame. Add rice and stir until rice is browned and saturated with oil. Add salt
and soy sauce and bouillon cubes, and cover with boiling water. Let simmer on
low heat for 30 minutes. Then add the water chestnuts, green onions, mushrooms, almonds, salt, and pepper. Return to a very low heat, and cook for an
additional 15 to 20 minutes until all the liquid is absorbed and the vegetables
are tender. Toss all ingredients before serving.

Serves 6 to 8

T *his rice dish may be served very comfortably with any of the Oriental recipes you may find on the pages of* Off the Top of My Stove.

Oriental Fried Rice

2	beaten eggs	1/4	cup finely chopped fresh mushrooms
3	tablespoons cooking oil	1/2	cup thinly sliced green onions
2	cups diced cooked pork *or* fully cooked ham	4	cups cooked rice
3	tablespoons soy sauce		Soy sauce

In a large skillet, cook the beaten eggs in 1 tablespoon of the oil, and scramble eggs till hard-cooked. Remove eggs. In same skillet, cook pork or ham, 3 tablespoons soy sauce, mushrooms, and green onion in remaining oil about 4 minutes or until mushrooms are tender. Stir in cooked rice and scrambled egg bits; heat through. Serve with additional soy sauce.

Serves 4 to 6

T *his is another dish I learned to cook at my mother's fingertips. It's the kind of dish where you can make a little or a lot without worrying about measuring every ounce that goes into the pan.*

A Bed of Red

1 1/2	pounds lean ground beef	1 1/2	cups long-grain rice
1	medium green pepper, seeded and chopped	1	cup chopped, peeled tomato
			14-ounce can tomato sauce
1/2	cup chopped onion	1	teaspoon fresh chili powder
1	clove garlic, minced	1	teaspoon salt
1	teaspoon Italian seasoning		Freshly ground black pepper
1/2	teaspoon dried rosemary, crushed	2 1/4	cups of water
2	tablespoons olive oil *or* cooking oil		

Brown the meat in a preheated, medium-sized skillet. Remove the meat and set aside. Pour off excess fat, and cook green pepper, onion, garlic, Italian seasoning, and rosemary in hot oil till vegetables are tender. Stir in rice, chopped tomato, tomato sauce, chili powder, salt, pepper, and 2 1/4 cups of water. Cook, covered, over low heat for about 15 minutes. Add meat, and cook through for an additional 5 minutes, stirring occasionally until the rice is tender.

Serves 6

B *ecause of the variety of flavors in this rice on the wild side, it is very tasty with the lighter meats such as veal or chicken.*

Nutty Wild Rice*

½ cup wild rice
1   cup long-grain rice
2   cups water
3   tablespoons of butter *or* margarine
1   teaspoon salt

½ cup slivered almonds
1   cup trail mix (raisins, pine nuts, walnuts, sunflower seeds)
Soy sauce

Cook wild rice according to package instructions. Combine long-grain rice, water, butter or margarine, and salt in a heavy 2-quart saucepan. Bring to a boil, reduce heat to low, and cover saucepan with a tight-fitting lid. Simmer, without lifting lid, 20 to 25 minutes or until rice is tender. Combine white rice with cooked wild rice and almonds and trail mix; toss lightly. Add a teaspoon or two of soy sauce, if desired.

Serves 4 to 5

"God gives the nuts, but He does not crack them."

German Proverb

*The term "wild rice" is really a misnomer. Wild rice is not actually rice, but a seed of a grass that grows in the Great Lakes region. Because it is so strong and rich in flavor, this recipe combines the wild rice with long-grained rice.

*T*o me, rice in any form will always be the "mother's milk" of all foods. It has a quality all its own, like getting a rubdown on the inside.

Sunny Risotto Lemonese

½ cup chopped onion
1   cup chopped summer squash
      (crookneck)
2   tablespoons butter *or* margarine
3   cups chicken broth
1½ cups long-grain rice
¼   teaspoon finely shredded lemon
      peel

¼   teaspoon salt
      Freshly ground black pepper
1   tablespoon lemon juice
½   cup Parmesan cheese
1   beaten egg
      8-ounce can stewed tomatoes

In a medium saucepan, cook onion and squash in butter or margarine until tender. Do not brown onion. Remove squash and set aside. Stir in broth, rice, lemon peel, salt, and pepper. Bring to a rolling boil, reduce heat to low. Cover tightly, and continue cooking for 15 minutes. Remove from heat and let rest for 5 to 8 minutes. Combine lemon juice, Parmesan cheese, and egg, and add to rice mixture. Add squash and stewed tomatoes. Cook over low heat 5 minutes to heat through, stirring gently. Serve immediately.

Serves 6

> "Tact consists in knowing how far to go in going too far."
>
> Jean Cocteau

*I*f you're out to impress someone, like your boss, maybe, serve this wonderful rice recipe with Stuffed Veal Rolls (p. 133), Broccoli with Lemon Sauce (p. 142), and an endive salad. If she brings the wine, keep your fingers crossed it's a Pouilly Fuisse or a Riesling.

Risotto Milanese

4   tablespoons butter *or* margarine
¼   cup finely chopped yellow onion
¼   cup finely chopped prosciutto
⅛   teaspoon saffron, crushed
3   cups beef broth

1½ cups long-grain rice
⅛   teaspoon salt
      Freshly ground pepper to taste
⅓   cup freshly grated Parmesan cheese

In 2 tablespoons butter or margarine, cook the onion with the prosciutto until the onion is tender but not brown. Add the saffron to the broth. Add the rice, broth, salt, and pepper to the prosciutto and onion. Bring to a boil and reduce heat to low. Cover tightly and cook for 15 minutes. Gently stir the risotto, and remove it from the heat to rest. If it's too dry, add a little more broth. The risotto should be tender, but still firm, and the mixture should be creamy. Stir in 2 tablespoons of butter and the ⅓ cup of Parmesan, and mix thoroughly. Spoon into a bowl, and serve with freshly ground Parmesan cheese on the side.

Serves 6

F or a very special occasion, serve Lobster Tails in Butter Sauce (p. 103) beside the risotto, and a salad of mixed greens, chopped green onions, and mushrooms with a creamy French dressing.

Razzle-Dazzle Risotto

2 cups broccoli flowerets	1½ cups long-grain rice
½ cup chopped celery	2 tablespoons snipped parsley
½ cup sliced green onions	⅛ teaspoon ground nutmeg
¼ cup finely chopped carrot	Freshly ground black pepper
1 clove garlic, minced	Grated Parmesan *or* Romano
2 tablespoons vegetable oil	cheese
3 cups chicken broth	

In a medium saucepan, cook broccoli, celery, onion, carrot, and garlic in cooking oil for 5 minutes or until vegetables are tender. Remove broccoli flowerets and set aside. Stir in chicken broth, rice, parsley, nutmeg, and pepper. Bring to a boil; reduce heat. Cover and simmer for 15 minutes. Remove from heat and let rest for 5 to 8 minutes or till rice is tender. Add broccoli flowerets and toss. Season to taste. Serve immediately. Pass Parmesan or Romano cheese.

Serves 6

R *isotto is how rice is prepared in some of the northern areas of Italy and simply means rice cooked in a seasoned broth until the mixture becomes creamy. Risotto is an easy and tasty alternative to pasta.*

Risotto & Chicken Livers

2   tablespoons butter *or* margarine
¾   cup finely chopped onion
3   cups canned chicken broth
¾   cup dry vermouth
1½ cups long-grain rice

1½ pounds fresh chicken livers
2   tablespoons olive oil
2   cloves garlic, crushed
    Freshly ground black pepper
    Paprika

In a heavy saucepan, heat butter or margarine over moderately low heat. Add onion and cook until tender, stirring frequently. Add broth and vermouth; cover and bring to a rolling boil. Add rice and reduce heat to a low temperature, and cook for 20 minutes. Remove from heat and let rest. Simultaneously, in a 10-inch skillet, cook chicken livers in oil and garlic until browned. Slice cooked livers in half and mix with rice. Dust with freshly ground black pepper, if desired. Fluff before serving. Sprinkle with paprika.

Serves 4

T *his rice dish is simple and tasty when served with Veal & Green Peppers (p. 135) and a green salad made with marinated artichoke hearts, sliced mushrooms, onion rounds, and romaine and iceberg lettuce, topped with a creamy garlic dressing.*

Risotto & Mushrooms

½   cup chopped onion
1   cup fresh sliced mushrooms
2   tablespoons butter *or* margarine
2¾ cups beef broth
¼   cup red wine

1½ cups long-grain rice
¼   teaspoon salt
    Freshly ground pepper
¼   cup Romano *or* Parmesan cheese

In a medium saucepan, cook onion and mushrooms in butter or margarine until tender, but not brown. Stir in broth, wine, rice, salt, and pepper. Bring to a rolling boil; reduce heat to low. Cover tightly, and continue cooking for 15 minutes (no peeking). Remove from heat and let rest, covered, for 5 to 8 minutes. Rice should be tender but still firm, and the mixture should be creamy. Stir in grated Romano or Parmesan cheese before serving.

Serves 6

Fish
The Basics

I can remember, once upon a time, when fish was served only once a week in my house. But since then we have grown more conscious of which foods are better for us. Seafood is a superb choice for weight control, and since there are so many varieties of fish in the ocean, we can not only be in good health, but we will never be bored.

Fish can be absolutely delicious, but it is and must be treated as a delicate food. Freshness is synonymous with quality in fish; however, present-day methods of quick-freezing fish are so good that the quality of frozen steaks and filets of many varieties is excellent. I mention this because in the hurly-burly of our western civilization, for some of us, frozen foods have become a way of life.

The only one sure thing we know about a fish is that it is the fastest-growing thing in nature. That is, from the time you catch it till the time you stop telling about it.

Before we begin to cook a fish, I'd like to tell you a little bit about the buying of fresh fish and also the storing of both fresh and frozen fish.

When buying whole or drawn fish, look for flesh that springs back when pressed; bright, clean eyes; tight, shining scales; and reddish pink gills.

When buying filets and steaks, look for flesh that appears freshly cut and has no browning around the edges. All fresh fish will have a fresh, mild odor.

When deciding upon quantity, count on one-third pound per person when serving steaks, filets, or fish sticks; one-half pound per person for dressed fish; and one pound per person for whole fish.

Fish spoils very easily; to avoid this, wrap fish in wax paper or put it in a tightly covered container. Store it immediately in the refrigerator, and cook it as soon as possible.

Frozen fish should be solidly frozen when purchased. There should be no ice crystals or discoloration and little or no odor.

To thaw fish, leave in its original wrapping, and place on a plate in the refrigerator. A pound of fish takes about 24 hours to thaw. *Do not* thaw fish at room temperature, and *do not* use warm water for thawing, as these methods may cause spoilage. A "faster" thawing process is to place the wrapped package of fish in *cold* water, changing the water frequently. A 16-ounce package takes about two hours to thaw. Use thawed fish within a day.

When it comes to cooking a fish, no matter what the recipe, no matter what the cooking method, there is one unalterable rule: *do not overcook*. You can judge doneness partly by appearance; when cooked, fish loses its translucence and becomes opaque. Also, when a fish is cooked, it flakes easily with a fork. Then you must remove it from the heat at once.

Fish falls into two classifications: lean or fat. White-fleshed fish such as sole, halibut, or cod are lean. Fish with colored flesh such as salmon or mackerel are fat. To prepare a lean fish, you may use a little more butter or oil. It is best to serve fish immediately after cooking, or it becomes dry and less flavorful.

These are some basic ways to cook fish off the top of your stove:

Pan-Fried   Frying is usually reserved for small, whole fish, such as trout, fish filets, steaks, and drawn fish. The fish may be breaded, if desired, by dipping in milk, then in breadcrumbs, corn meal, or flour. Use melted shortening to cover the bottom of the pan. Fry fish until light brown, turn, and brown other side. Use a moderate temperature to fry fish.

Poached or Boiled   Tie the fish in a length of cheesecloth, place it on the flat, greased tray of a fish poacher or a large skillet and cover the fish with a seasoned liquid. Simmer gently until the fish flakes easily. Remove it from the hot liquid immediately. As the poaching liquid, you may choose to use wine or a fish stock. These liquids can be reduced and used as a sauce to serve with the fish.

Steamed   Steaming is similar to poaching except that the fish is cooked over the liquid instead of in it. Place the fish in a deep pan on a greased, perforated rack that will hold it above the level of the liquid. Bring the liquid to a boil, and cover the pan tightly. Cook just until fish flakes easily. Season and salt fish after steaming.

> *"Never a fisherman need there be, if fishes could hear as well as see."*
>
> Anonymous

*C*reamy Home Made Coleslaw (p. 147) is a tasty complement to any fried fish dish, and for the vegetable, serve Sautéed Zucchini (p. 158). This combination never misses! As an added suggestion, mix 2 cups ketchup with ½ cup horseradish, and let your guests help themselves.

Flaky Fried Fish

2 pounds boneless fish, cut into serving-size pieces about 1½ inches thick	⅛ teaspoon hot sauce
	½ cup flour
	¼ teaspoon salt
Garlic salt	½ teaspoon dry mustard
1 egg	Vegetable oil
⅓ cup milk	

Rinse fish and pat dry with paper towels. Sprinkle lightly with garlic salt, if desired, and set aside. In a bowl beat egg slightly, then stir in milk and hot sauce. Mix together flour, salt, and mustard. Stir into egg mixture and beat until smooth. In a heavy deep saucepan or electric skillet, have oil at least 1½ inches deep, and heat over moderate flame. Coat fish with batter, and fry 3 to 5 minutes on each side, or until well-browned and fish flakes easily with fork.

Serves 4 to 6

"In still waters are the largest fish."
Danish Proverb

*A*n unusual side dish to serve with the cod would be Whipped Sweet Potatoes & Parsnips (p. 161), topped off with Green Beans Amandine (p. 153) and a crunchy loaf of warmed sourdough bread.

Codfish Español

1½ pounds cod	2 tablespoons chopped pimiento
1 large onion, sliced thinly in rings	Dash pepper
1 clove garlic, minced	⅓ cup dry sherry
¼ cup cooking oil	¼ cup sliced pimiento-stuffed olives
16-ounce can tomatoes, cut up	

Cut cod into serving-size pieces. Cook onion and garlic in oil till onion is tender but not brown. Add fish pieces and cook till lightly browned. Add undrained tomatoes, pimiento, and pepper. Simmer, uncovered, about 20 minutes or till fish is tender. Add sherry; heat through. Garnish with olives.

Serves 4

*B*ecause the sauce for this recipe is so elegant, I prefer to keep the combination offered fairly simple. So marry this dish with Risotto & Mushrooms (p. 82) or Parsley New Potatoes (p. 156) and Green Beans Amandine (p. 156). A dry white zinfandel will round out the dinner perfectly.

Filet of Sole Veronica

2	pounds sole filets	1	tablespoon sherry
1½	cups water	1	teaspoon lemon juice
1	cup dry white wine		Salt and pepper to taste
1	medium onion, quartered	1	cup well-drained canned seedless
1	bay leaf		grapes *or* 1½ cups fresh seedless
3–4	whole peppercorns		grapes poached in white wine for
½	teaspoon salt		5 minutes
1	cup cream		

Rinse fish with cold water; pat dry with paper towels. In large skillet, combine water, wine, onion, bay leaf, peppercorns, and ½ teaspoon salt. Bring to boil; reduce heat. Add fish to liquid; cover and simmer for 4 to 5 minutes, or until fish flakes easily when tested with a fork. Drain fish, reserving cooking liquid. Place fish on platter and keep warm. Strain reserved liquid; return to skillet. Add butter and flour and boil rapidly until reduced to ¾ cup. Remove from heat. Gradually add cream to reduced liquid. Continue cooking over medium heat until mixture thickens. Mix in sherry, lemon juice, salt, and pepper. Stir in grapes. Pour hot sauce over fish. Serve immediately.

Serves 6

*M*y mother would always say, "Eat your fish; it's brain food." I like to think she was right!

Filet of Sole Amandine

1½	pounds filet of sole	3	tablespoons sliced blanched
	Salt and pepper		almonds
4	tablespoons butter *or* margarine		Lemon wedges
2	tablespoons butter *or* margarine		Parsley

Cut fish into serving-size portions, and sprinkle with salt and pepper. Heat the 4 tablespoons butter in a large skillet over moderate heat. Add fish and cook until lightly browned on both sides, about 8 minutes. (Add additional butter if necessary.) Remove fish to a warm platter. Add the remaining 2 tablespoons butter and increase temperature to moderately high; add almonds and cook until lightly browned. Pour over fish and garnish with lemon wedges and parsley.

Serves 4

This sole-food dish is at its best with the following sauce:

Wine-Butter Sauce

¼ cup butter *or* margarine
½ cup white wine
1 tablespoon lemon juice

1 tablespoon chopped parsley
¼ salt

Melt ¼ cup butter or margarine in a saucepan over low heat. Stir in ½ cup white wine, 1 tablespoon lemon juice, 1 tablespoon chopped parsley, and ¼ teaspoon salt. Heat before serving. Makes ¾ cup sauce.

F or a match made in heaven, serve these roll-ups with Linguine with White Clam Sauce (p. 52). Then sit back and sip a glass of Chardonnay.

Fish Filets & Asparagus Roll-Ups

4 fresh or frozen flounder or sole
   filets
¾ pound fresh asparagus
   Salt
1 tablespoon butter *or* margarine
2 medium tomatoes, peeled and cut
   up
½ cup sliced fresh mushrooms

¼ cup thinly sliced celery
¼ cup chopped onion
¼ cup dry white wine
1 clove garlic, minced
½ teaspoon dried mint, crushed
½ teaspoon dried basil, crushed
¼ teaspoon salt

Thaw fish, if frozen. Cut fresh asparagus into 6-inch lengths. Place asparagus in a steamer basket and cook, covered, over a small pot of boiling water for about 8 minutes, till almost tender.

Drain. Sprinkle filets with salt, and dot with butter or margarine. Place asparagus across filets; roll up filets and fasten with wooden picks. Place fish roll-ups, seam side down, in 10-inch skillet. Add tomatoes, mushrooms, celery, onion, wine, garlic, dried mint, basil, and ¼ teaspoon salt. Cover tightly; simmer for 8 minutes or till fish flakes easily with a fork. Remove fish to platter; keep warm. Boil tomato mixture gently, uncovered, about 3 minutes or till slightly thickened. Spoon over fish rolls. Serve immediately.

Serves 4

". . . I stick to asparagus which still seems to inspire gentle thoughts."

Charles Lamb

*M*y father was a devoted fish fancier and enjoyed this rich, tasty dish accompanied by thin egg noodles, Broccoli with Lemon Sauce (p. 142), and a wedge of iceberg lettuce with French dressing.

Halibut & Mushrooms in White Wine Sauce

6	fresh *or* frozen halibut steaks	½	cup dry white wine
1	medium carrot, chopped	½	teaspoon dried thyme, crushed
1	stalk celery, chopped	½	pound mushrooms, sliced
1	medium onion, chopped	2	slightly beaten egg yolks
2	tablespoons butter *or* margarine	½	cup heavy cream
1	chicken bouillon cube, dissolved in 1 cup hot water		Salt and pepper

Thaw fish, if frozen. In a large skillet, cook carrot, celery, and onion in butter or margarine until just tender. Place fish on top of vegetables in skillet. Add broth, wine, and thyme. Cover and simmer for 5 to 10 minutes or till fish flakes easily with a fork. Remove fish to a platter and keep warm.

Strain the pan liquid; return to skillet. Boil, uncovered, over high heat for 1 to 2 minutes or till reduced to 1 cup. Reduce heat. Add mushrooms to skillet. Combine egg yolks and heavy cream. Mix and stir into mushroom mixture in skillet. Cook and stir till thickened. Season to taste with salt and pepper. Spoon sauce over fish.

Serves 6

"Ann, Ann!
Come! quick as you can!
There's a fish that talks
in the frying pan."

Walter De La Mare

*A*n *unusual match here is to serve Whipped Sweet Potatoes & Parsnips (p. 161) and Buttered Green Beans & Water Chestnuts (p. 143). Your guests and the haddock will be genuinely pleased.*

Poached Haddock in Mustard Sauce

1 tablespoon lemon juice	1 teaspoon vinegar
4 peppercorns	1 teaspoon salt
1 bay leaf	1½ pound haddock steaks
1 cup water	Mustard Sauce (recipe follows)
1 small onion, thinly sliced	

Place all ingredients except fish and Mustard Sauce in a saucepan, bring to a boil over low heat and simmer 5 minutes. Strain stock into a large skillet; add fish and simmer 10 to 15 minutes, or until fish is easily flaked. Remove fish to platter and keep warm. Strain broth and use in Mustard Sauce.

Serves 4

Mustard Sauce

1 tablespoon vegetable oil	Fish stock
1 tablespoon finely chopped onion	Milk
1 tablespoon flour	1 tablespoon prepared mustard

Heat oil in saucepan over moderate heat; add onion and cook until tender. Blend in flour and cook 1 minute. Measure fish stock and add enough milk to make 1 cup liquid. Gradually, stir stock into flour mixture. Cook, stirring constantly, until thickened. Blend in mustard.

Makes 1 cup sauce

"Oh, you who've been a fishing
Will endorse me when I say,
That it always is the biggest fish
You catch that gets away!"

Eugene Field

I *like to let my imagination run away with me, and take me to a running brook, surrounded by the sounds and sights of Mother Nature doing her majestic thing, while we stand silently, knee-deep in water, waiting to hook one of her silver splendors.*

Trout Meunière

¼	cup flour	1	tablespoon chopped fresh parsley
½	teaspoon salt	¼	teaspoon dried tarragon leaves
4	brook trout, about ¾ pounds each	1	teaspoon grated lemon peel
	Salt and pepper	2	tablespoons lemon juice
½	cup butter *or* margarine		

Mix flour and salt. Sprinkle insides of trout with salt and pepper. Dredge trout in flour mixture. Melt half of the butter in skillet over moderate heat. Add fish and brown well, about 5 minutes on each side. Remove to warm platter. Add the remaining butter, parsley, tarragon, lemon peel, and lemon juice; heat until butter foams. Serve over trout.

Serves 4

T *his dish is exceptional when served with Asparagus and Pasta (p. 48), an endive salad, and crusty whole wheat French bread.*

Poached Halibut in Clam Sauce

2	pounds halibut steak (½ pound per person)	4	cloves garlic, sliced
2	cups water	2	6½-ounce cans minced *or* chopped clams, drained, *or* 1 pint shucked littleneck clams
2	cups dry white wine		Red pepper flakes
1	small onion sliced	2	tablespoons chopped parsley
1	bay leaf	1	bottle clam juice (if using canned clams)
10	whole peppercorns		
½	teaspoon salt		
⅓	cup olive oil		

To cook the fish, place the steaks in a poaching liquid of half water and half white wine in which a few slices of onion, bay leaf, peppercorns, and salt have simmered till onion is tender. Be sure the liquid covers the fish. Once the fish has been added, adjust the heat so the liquid barely shivers. Cook the halibut for five minutes, then turn off the heat and cover. Allow the fish to stand in the liquid for 20 minutes before serving. It will not overcook.

For the clam sauce: Heat ⅓ cup olive oil and the garlic in a saucepan. Cook over medium heat until the garlic turns golden brown. Add the clams. (Note: If using shucked clams, be sure they are chopped.) Add a pinch of red pepper flakes and the parsley. Then add the clam juice.

*I*nstead of barbecuing again, why not make this dish on an early August evening, served with a Summer Squash Medley (p. 160) and pitchers of mimosa punch? Your guests will be happy you did!

Poached Sunshine Sole

2	tablespoons dry sherry	2	pounds frozen sole filets *or* flounder, thawed
1	tablespoon soy sauce		Salt
1	cup orange juice	½	cup cold water
4	medium carrots, thinly sliced	2	teaspoons cornstarch
1	medium onion, sliced and separated into rings	1	tomato, cut into 8 wedges
1	medium green pepper, cut into strips		

In a large skillet, combine dry sherry, soy sauce, and orange juice. Add carrots and onion; bring to a boil. Reduce heat; simmer, covered, for 8 minutes, until vegetables are crisp-tender. Add green pepper, and push vegetables to rim of skillet.

Season fish with salt; place in center of skillet, and bring to a boil. Reduce heat and simmer, covered, 2 to 3 minutes until fork-tender. Remove fish from skillet. Combine the cold water and cornstarch, and add to skillet. Cook and stir till thickened. Return fish to skillet; arrange tomato wedges on top. Heat through and serve immediately.

This is a wonderful dish to serve with brown rice.

Serves 4

*T*he only thing that may be lacking in this flavorful "meal-in-one" is a tossed
green salad and a cool glass of white wine.

Sautéed Potato & Fish Dish

2	medium potatoes, thinly sliced		Sprinkling of pepper
2	medium carrots, julienned	2	tablespoons butter *or* margarine
1	small onion, thinly sliced into rings	1	tablespoon vegetable oil
1/4	teaspoon salt	1 1/2	pounds frozen haddock, flounder, *or*
1/4	teaspoon garlic powder		perch filets, thawed and cut into
1/4	teaspoon dry mustard		2-inch pieces
1/4	teaspoon celery seasoning	2	tablespoons snipped parsley

In a large skillet, cook the vegetables in a small amount of water, covered,
about 10 minutes or just till tender; drain. Combine salt, garlic powder, mustard, celery seasoning, and pepper. Add butter or margarine to vegetables in
skillet; sprinkle with salt mixture. Toss gently till the butter is melted and vegetables are coated. Remove them to a platter; wrap in foil to keep warm.

Add cooking oil to skillet; add fish pieces to hot oil. Cook, uncovered, over
medium heat 5 to 10 minutes or till fish flakes easily with a fork. Turn fish
once during cooking. Arrange fish on platter with vegetables. Sprinkle with
parsley.

Serves 4

*"A codfish lays 10,000 eggs in a single day, but it is
done silently. A hen lays one egg and cackles. Nobody
eats codfish eggs, and nearly everybody eats chicken
eggs."*
George Bernard Shaw

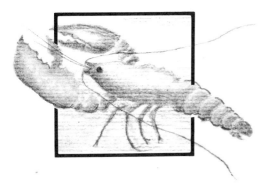

Shellfish
The Basics

S hellfish, the little darlings of the fish family, include crab, shrimp, and lobster (the crustaceans), and clams, oysters, and scallops (the mollusks). Many people who claim that fish is not their cup of tea will, most enthusiastically, order a shrimp cocktail for an appetizer.

All shellfish are low in calories and high in nutrients—a highly desirable combination. They are extremely delicate, and when bought fresh, must be kept ice-cold until cooked. Frozen shellfish should not be thawed until you are ready to cook it, and once it is thawed, it should not be refrozen.

"Let us royster with the oyster—in the shorter days
  and moister
That are brought by brown September, with its
  roguish final 'R';*
For breakfast, or for supper, on the under shell or
  upper,
Of dishes he's the daisy, and of shell-fish, he's the
  star."

Anonymous

*Refers to those months of the year, May through August, which are "R" less.

Clams

C lams can be purchased in the shell by the pound, or shucked by the pint or quart. When buying shell clams, they should be alive, the shells unbroken and tightly closed; if the clam inside is alive, an open shell will close quickly when touched. Shucked clams should be plump, with clear liquid and a good fresh odor.

Small hard-shelled clams, such as littlenecks and cherrystones, are most often served raw on the half-shell or are cooked in most recipes. Large hard-shelled clams such as quahogs and chowders are used in chowder and other recipes. Soft-shelled clams are used for steaming. The smallest and the sweetest clams are known as "steamers." Razor clams, which only come in canned form, are used for clam bisque or chowder.

Unless you plan on using the shell in your recipe, it is easier to buy clams already shucked, either fresh, canned, or frozen. For six main-dish portions, you will need about a quart of shucked clams, three dozen shell clams, or two 6½-ounce cans.

T he texture and the taste of hot, crunchy bread dipped into the clam broth reminds me of dining at Gosman's Restaurant on the tip of Montauk Point, where the seagulls would swoop down, hoping to catch a morsel of food in midair!

Clams & White Wine Broth

60 fresh *or* frozen clams in the shell	1 clove garlic, minced
1½ cups chicken broth	1 tablespoon dried mint, crushed
1½ cups dry white wine	1 teaspoon dried basil, crushed
½ cup sliced green onion	½ teaspoon dried oregano, crushed
⅓ cup snipped parsley	2 tablespoons snipped parsley

If clams are frozen, thaw. Thoroughly wash clams in shells. Cover with salted water (⅓ cup salt to one gallon water); let stand for about 15 minutes; rinse. Repeat this process two more times.

In a large kettle or Dutch oven, combine chicken broth, wine, green onions, 1/3 cup snipped parsley, garlic, mint, basil, and oregano. Bring to a boil; add clams. Reduce heat; cover and simmer for about 10 to 15 minutes or till clams open.

Remove clams from liquid, and discard any that do not open. Strain and reserve the liquid. Add 2 tablespoons snipped parsley to strained liquid. Serve clams and liquid in separate individual bowls; dip clams into broth before eating.

Serves 4

"Peace is happiness digesting."
Victor Hugo

*W*hen it comes to fried seafood, I always think of Creamy Home Made Coleslaw (p. 147) and pots of corn on the cob. Sip a cold beer in a chilled mug, and count the seagulls flying overhead.

Fried Clams

1 quart shucked clams	1 teaspoon pepper
3 eggs	1½ cups fine dry bread crumbs
3 tablespoons milk	Vegetable oil for frying
1½ teaspoons salt	

Drain clams. You may reserve liquid for use in soups or clam sauce. Dry clams well between paper towels. Beat together eggs, milk, salt, and pepper. Dip clams in egg mixture and then in bread crumbs. Recoat with egg and bread crumbs. Prick clams several times with a fork. Let stand 30 minutes before frying. In a deep skillet or deep-fat fryer, heat oil for frying until hot, then place 4 to 5 clams at a time into the fat. Fry about 5 minutes, until golden brown. Drain well on paper towels.

Serves 6

T hese little thin-shelled steamers, or "piss-clams" as they are called on the Eastern seaboard, are, to me, the sweetest in flavor of the clam set. Serve Bloody Marys all around, with hot bread to dip with and good friends to laugh with.

Screaming Steamed Clams

6	pounds steamers *or* littleneck clams	$\frac{1}{2}$	teaspoon oregano
	Water	1	tablespoon celery seasoning
2	tablespoons parsley flakes		Melted butter or margarine

Scrub clams thoroughly. Heat 1 inch of water in large Dutch oven to boiling. Add clams, parsley flakes, oregano, and celery seasoning. Cover and cook over moderate heat 15 minutes or until shells open. (Discard clams with unopened shells.) Serve with strained broth, and dip in melted butter.

Serves 6

Crab

C rabs are either soft-shelled or hard-shelled. Soft-shell crabs are available in the warm months, from May to October. Fresh hard-shelled crabs are available year-round. Soft-shell crabs are found all along the Atlantic coastline and have bright blue claws.

Dungeness crab is taken from the Pacific coast waters, while rock crab is caught off the New England and sunny California shores. Alaska king crab comes from the northern Pacific, and only the leg meat is eaten.

There are various grades of cooked crabmeat for sale on your market shelves. There's lump meat, with solid pieces from the body of the crab; flake meat, or small pieces from the rest of the body; lump and flake meat combined; and claw meat. Lump meat is the most attractive and the most expensive. Live hard-shelled crabs are sold only in the areas where they are caught, so more than likely, you will be purchasing soft-shell crabs for your recipes. Two per person is adequate. One pound of crab meat will make six main-course portions or eight to ten appetizer portions.

Soft-shell crabs are usually cleaned by your local fish market and are sold ready to cook.

T *hese little party crab cakes do the best disappearing act in town—so I usually double the recipe! When the first batch is almost gone, and before the last few guests arrive, I put the second batch on the fire.*

Oriental Crab Cakes

1 tablespoon butter or margarine	Salt and pepper to taste
1 tablespoon flour	1/2 cup cornstarch
1/2 cup milk	Vegetable oil
3 green onions, thinly sliced	Chinese hot mustard
7 1/2-ounce can crab meat, drained, broken into chunks, and cartilage removed	Soy sauce

Melt butter, then add flour and stir, making a roux; then add milk slowly to make a thick cream sauce. Bring to a boil, adding green onions, crab meat, and salt and pepper. Form into small squares. Roll in cornstarch and deep fry in vegetable oil. Drain on paper towels. Serve hot with Chinese hot mustard and soy sauce.

Makes 25

*W*henever I make this dish, I see a crab wearing a large sombrero, chewing on a cigar, and waving a gun, saying, "C'mon, make my day."

Crab Tostadas

	Vegetable oil	2	canned green chile peppers, rinsed, seeded, and chopped
8	6-inch flour tortillas	1	small avocado
1	tablespoon lime juice	2	cups shredded lettuce
1	tablespoon olive oil	1	tomato, chopped and drained
1/4	teaspoon salt		Lime wedges
	Dash pepper		Hot pepper sauce
	7 1/2-ounce can crab meat, drained, flaked, and cartilage removed		

In heavy skillet, heat 1/4 inch oil. Fry tortillas, one at a time, in hot oil for 20 to 40 seconds on each side or till crisp and golden. Drain on paper toweling. Keep warm in foil.

Mix together lime juice, olive oil, and salt and pepper. Toss with crab and chile peppers. Divide mixture among tortillas. Seed, peel, and cube avocado. Top crab and peppers with lettuce, tomato, and avocado. Pass lime wedges and hot pepper sauce.

Makes 8 servings

*T*his lovely dish can be made in the smallest of galleys and served on deck with a tossed green salad, sesame bread sticks, and flutes of chilled champagne.

Crabmeat Marinara

2	tablespoons olive oil	3	whole peppercorns
1	small chopped onion		Few grains cayenne pepper
1	tablespoon dried parsley flakes	3	pounds fresh tomatoes
1 1/4	teaspoons dried basil leaves		Boiling water
1/2	teaspoon sugar	2	7 1/4-ounce cans Alaska king crab meat, drained and flaked
2	teaspoons salt		
1/4	teaspoon garlic powder	3	cups cooked noodles

Place olive oil, onion, parsley, basil, sugar, salt, garlic powder, peppercorns, and cayenne in a large saucepan or Dutch oven. Dip tomatoes into boiling water for 1 minute; remove from water, cut out stem end, and remove skin. Dice tomatoes and add to seasonings in pan. Place over moderate heat and cook 20 to 30 minutes, or until sauce is well-blended and slightly thickened, stirring constantly. Add crab and heat over moderately low heat for 5 minutes. Serve over noodles.

Serves 6

T *his* Off-the-Top-of-My-Stove *summer casserole dish proves most enjoyable when served with a platter of sliced honeydew and crenshaw melon, and a bowl of fresh spinach salad with mushroom slices and egg quarters, topped with a creamy bacon dressing.*

Crabby Rice Skillet

3/4 cup long-grain rice
1   small onion, finely chopped
1   small clove garlic, minced
2   tablespoons cooking oil
1¼ cups water
     8-ounce can tomatoes, cut up
1   chicken bouillon cube

¼   teaspoon salt
     Hot pepper sauce
½   cup frozen peas
     7½-ounce can crab meat, drained, broken into chunks, and cartilage removed
2   tablespoons dry sherry

In large skillet, cook rice, onion, and garlic in oil over medium-low heat, stirring occasionally, till rice is golden-brown. Remove from heat. Add water, *undrained* tomatoes, bouillon cube, salt, and a few dashes of the hot pepper sauce. Cover and simmer about 15 minutes or till most of liquid is absorbed. Stir in peas; cook 5 minutes more. Stir in crab and sherry; heat through.

Serves 4

Try the Tortellini Salad (p. 63) with these dazzlers from the depths, and wedges of fresh pineapple.

Fried Soft-Shelled Crabs

12 soft-shelled crabs	¾ cup flour
2 eggs, beaten	¾ fine bread crumbs
¼ cup milk	Oil for frying
2 teaspoons salt	

Have crabs cleaned at the fish market. Rinse in cold water; drain and dry between paper towels. Combine eggs, milk, and salt. Mix flour and crumbs. Dip crabs in egg mixture and then roll in flour-crumb mixture. In a large skillet, heat oil over moderate heat. Add crabs and cook until browned on both sides, about 8 to 10 minutes. Drain on paper towels.

Serves 6

Tartar Sauce

½ cup mayonnaise *or* salad dressing	2 tablespoons chopped dill pickle
¼ cup commercial sour cream	½ teaspoon dried tarragon leaves
2 tablespoons chopped fresh parsley	

Fold together all ingredients. Makes about ¾ cup sauce

"We may live without poetry, music and art;
We may live without conscience and live without heart;
We may live without friends, we may live without books;
But civilized man cannot live without cooks."

Owen Meredith

Lobster

Northern lobster, caught in the cold Atlantic waters, is in season all year, but is most plentiful in the summer months. The rock lobster, sometimes referred to as "spiny," is found in the warmer waters around Florida and California; in certain areas, the rock lobster is always in season.

Live Northern lobsters should have a dark bluish-green shell. They must be alive when you buy them, and the tail should curl quickly under the body when they are picked up. Cooked lobsters have a bright red shell. The tail should spring back under the body when straightened out, proving that the lobster was alive just before it was cooked.

A one-pound live lobster or a five- to eight-ounce lobster tail will be enough for one dinner serving. One-half pound of cooked lobster meat will serve as appetizer for six. Two one-pound live lobsters will yield one-half pound cooked meat. When preparing a recipe, bear in mind that it is easier to buy cooked lobster meat (fresh, canned, or frozen), and it eliminates any guilt feeling you may have about plunging that defenseless critter into a pot of boiling water.

When serving lobster, make sure the table is spacious with room for crackers, forks, butter dipping bowls, bowls for cracked shells, salad and salad bowls, breadsticks, wine and wine glasses, and lots of napkins. Also have on hand new, colorful dish towels which your guests can choose to wear as bibs.

Boiled Lobster

4	1- to 1½-pound live lobsters	6	tablespoons salt
6	quarts boiling water		Melted butter

Plunge lobsters headfirst into a large pot of boiling salted water. Cover and return to boiling point; reduce heat and simmer over low heat about 20 minutes. Drain. Place lobsters on their backs, and cut in half lengthwise with a sharp knife. Remove the head and the stomach (which is right behind the head) and the dark vein that runs from the stomach to the tip of the tail. Do not discard the green liver and coral roe. Crack claws with a lobster cracker and provide small forks for removing the meat. Serve with melted butter.

Serves 4

Did you know that lobsters can fly? Almost everyday, in seaports from New England to Montauk Bay, they get together and take flight, landing all across the country.

Citrus Lobster Salad

4   large oranges
1¼ cups cooked lobster, broken into
    pieces
1   cup thinly sliced celery

¼ cup salad dressing *or* mayonnaise
¼ teaspoon salt
1   head leafy lettuce
2   teaspoons thinly sliced green onion

Cut slice from top of each orange. Remove fruit from oranges, leaving shells. Discard orange tops. Chop fruit. Cut top edge of each orange shell in saw-tooth fashion. Place shells in plastic bag and refrigerate. In a mixing bowl, combine chopped orange, lobster, and celery; chill. Stir together salad dressing (or mayonnaise) and salt. Drain lobster mixture; add to salad dressing mixture and toss. Line orange shells with lettuce; spoon in lobster mixture. Place filled orange cups on lettuce-lined plates. Garnish with green onion.

Serves 4

T his romantic midnight dinner need only be served with candlelight, rice, and champagne—in that order—followed by a kiss.

Lobster Newburg

1	tablespoon butter *or* margarine	⅓	cup heavy cream
1	cup cooked lobster meat (frozen lobster tails may be used)	¼	teaspoon salt
1	tablespoon dry sherry		Few grains cayenne pepper
1	egg yolk		Few grains ground nutmeg

Melt butter or margarine in a saucepan over moderate heat; add lobster meat pieces and cook 3 minutes. Add sherry and heat 1 minute. Beat egg yolk and cream together; gradually stir into lobster mixture. Cook over low heat, stirring constantly, until sauce just starts to thicken, about 4 to 5 minutes. (If sauce boils, it will separate.) Stir in salt, cayenne, and nutmeg.

Serves 2

I wonder if lobsters know how expensive they are? And if they do, if they care?

Lobster Tails in Butter Sauce

4	frozen lobster tails	½	teaspoon salt
⅓	cup butter *or* margarine,		Freshly ground pepper
1	clove garlic, minced	⅓	cup chopped fresh parsley
½	teaspoon dried oregano leaves, crushed		Parmesan cheese

Cook lobster tails in boiling salted water 6 to 8 minutes, or until tender; drain and cool. Cut membrane along both edges of shell and remove membrane. Lift meat out of shells, and reserve shells. Dice lobster meat coarsely. Melt butter in skillet over moderate heat and mix in garlic, oregano, salt, and pepper. Add lobster meat and cook until heated. Fold in parsley and spoon into lobster shells. Sprinkle with Parmesan cheese.

Serves 4

Oysters

A lthough oysters are available year-round, the best season is from the first of September to the first of May. From coast to coast, every state which borders on the sea, with the exception of Maine and New Hampshire, has an abundance of oysters.

Oysters are sold raw by the dozen, in the shell or on the half-shell; or shucked by the pint or quart. They are also sold canned or frozen. If you plan to cook them, it is easier to buy them already shucked. If you buy them in the shell, they should be alive, the shell tightly closed. The oyster should be plump, shiny, and fresh-smelling. For six main-dish portions, you'll need three dozen oysters in the shell or one quart of shucked oysters.

I n Los Angeles, salads are served in bowls you can eat! I may be missing the point, but I prefer to serve my salads in china—bowls, that is!

Shellfish Salad

1	medium head lettuce	½	cup salad oil
	8-ounce can whole oysters, drained	½	cup vinegar
	16-ounce package frozen cooked	2	teaspoons dried dill weed
	shrimp, thawed	¾	teaspoon sugar
	5-ounce can lobster, drained, broken	¾	teaspoon salt
	into large pieces with cartilage	½	teaspoon horseradish
	removed	3	medium tomatoes, cut into wedges
2	cups sliced fresh mushrooms	1	lemon, cut into 8 wedges
½	cup celery		

In a large salad bowl, toss together the lettuce, drained oysters, shrimp, lobster pieces, sliced mushrooms, and celery. In screw-top jar combine the salad oil, vinegar, dill weed, sugar, salt, and horseradish. Shake well.

Pour oil mixture over lettuce-seafood mixture. Toss to coat well. Add the tomato wedges and toss gently. Garnish each serving with a lemon wedge.

Serves 8

F or a bountiful dish, try doubling this recipe served with a tossed green salad and lots of grog. You may prevent a mutiny.

Oyster Fritter-Critters

1	pint fresh *or* frozen oysters, drained and chopped	2	egg yolks
1½	cups sifted flour	¼	cup reserved oyster liquor
2	teaspoons baking powder	1	tablespoon vegetable oil
¾	teaspoon salt	¼	teaspoon paprika
2	egg whites		Vegetable oil for frying

Drain 1 pint oysters and reserve ¼ cup of the liquor. Coarsely chop oysters. Sift together flour, baking powder, and salt. Beat egg whites until stiff peaks form. Beat egg yolks, ¼ cup of oyster liquor, and 1 tablespoon vegetable oil together until blended. Add sifted dry ingredients with paprika and beat until smooth. Fold in egg whites and chopped oysters. In a large skillet, pour in oil, and heat over moderate high heat. Spoon ¼ cup of batter into hot fat and fry 10 minutes, allowing 5 minutes on each side. Drain on paper towels.

Makes about 12 fritters

I f you're planning a fish fry out on the deck, cook up a combination of fried oysters, clams, batter-fried fish, and butterfly shrimp. Have bowls of tartar sauce and cocktail sauce for dipping, iced drinks, and warm friends to share it with!

Overboard Oysters

1	quart frying-size oysters	Few grains pepper
3	eggs	1½ cups seasoned bread crumbs
3	tablespoons milk	Vegetable oil for frying
1½	teaspoons salt	

Drain oysters. Dry oysters well between paper towels. Beat together eggs, milk, salt and pepper. Dip oysters in egg mixture and then in bread crumbs. Recoat with eggs and bread crumbs. Allow oysters to stand 30 minutes before frying. Heat oil in a Dutch oven. When oil is hot, gradually lower 4 to 5 oysters at a time into the fat. Fry about 5 minutes, until golden brown. Drain well on paper towels.

Serves 4

Scallops

There are two types of scallops: bay scallops, found in inshore waters from New England to the Gulf of Mexico; and sea scallops, which are brought in from the deep waters off the Northern and Middle Atlantic states. Sea scallops are large, sometimes as big as two inches in diameter. Bay scallops are small, and are especially tender and sweet.

Bay scallops are only sold fresh, while sea scallops are sold both fresh and frozen. Both types should have a sweet odor and be free from liquid. One pound of scallops will serve three to four. Scallops are ready for use just as you buy them. Rinse them in cold water and dry thoroughly.

It's 3 A.M., and I can almost see the bare electric bulbs shining like little moons in the stalls of the Fulton Fish market. Then, if you knew someone, and I did, you could always buy the pick of the catch, catch a cab, hit the highway, and think of friends to invite for Sunday brunch.

Scallops & Pasta Shells

1	pound fresh bay scallops	1/8	teaspoon pepper
1	cup chopped onion	1	cup tomatoes, peeled, seeded, and chopped
2	tablespoons butter *or* margarine		
1	tablespoon olive oil	12	ounces conchiglie (medium-size shells), cooked
1	cup dry white wine		
1	chicken bouillon cube	1/4	cup butter *or* margarine, melted
1	teaspoon dried basil, crushed	1/2	cup grated Parmesan cheese
1/2	teaspoon salt	1/2	cup snipped parsley

Wash scallops, and cut in half. In saucepan, cook onion in 2 tablespoons butter or margarine and the olive oil till tender but not brown. Stir in wine, bouillon cube, basil, 1/2 teaspoon salt, and 1/8 teaspoon pepper. Bring to a boil; reduce heat. Boil gently, uncovered, for 12 to 15 minutes or till about 2/3 of the liquid is evaporated. Add scallops to the wine mixture. Cover and simmer for about 5 minutes or till scallops are tender. Stir in chopped tomatoes and heat through. Toss cooked shells with 1/4 cup melted butter or margarine. Add scallop mixture, cheese, and parsley; toss till pasta is coated.

Serves 4

*T*his rich, creamy dish is delightful accompanied by Asparagus Vinaigrette (p. 140) and a warmed loaf of Italian bread. For a definitive tasting wine, try a Riesling or a Macon-Villages.

Scallops Tetrazzini

1 pound fresh *or* frozen scallops	1/2 teaspoon salt
1 1/2 cups water	1/2 teaspoon dry mustard
1 tablespoon lemon juice	Dash pepper
1/4 teaspoon salt	1 cup milk
1 bay leaf	4 small mushrooms, sliced
2 tablespoons sliced green onion	2 tablespoons dry sherry
3 tablespoons butter *or* margarine	8 ounces vermicelli, broken
1/4 cup flour	1/4 cup grated Parmesan cheese

Thaw scallops in the refrigerator overnight, if frozen. In saucepan, combine scallops, water, lemon juice, salt, and bay leaf. Bring to a boil. Reduce heat and simmer 2 to 3 minutes. Remove scallops and cool; slice. Discard bay leaf, reserve 1/2 cup of cooking liquid.

For the sauce, in a saucepan, cook the 2 tablespoons of green onion in butter or margarine till tender. Stir in flour, salt, dry mustard, and pepper. Stir in the milk and the reserved cooking liquid. Cook and stir till thickened. Cook and stir 1 to 2 minutes more. Stir in the mushrooms, sherry, and scallops.

Cook vermicelli 5 to 6 minutes, till tender. Drain. Top vermicelli with scallop mixture, and sprinkle with Parmesan cheese.

Serves 4

"But four young oysters hurried up,
All eager for the treat:
Their coats were brushed, their faces washed
Their shoes were clean and neat—
And this was odd, because, you know,
They hadn't any feet."
Lewis Carroll

I like to think of this dish as the "Body Beautiful" dish—because I don't serve it with anything else. Oh, maybe a lettuce leaf or two.

Sautéed Scallops & Shrimp in White Wine

1½ pounds medium fresh shrimp
1½ pounds fresh bay scallops
3 tablespoons lemon juice
6 tablespoons olive oil
½ teaspoon dried oregano leaves, crushed

3 cloves garlic, finely minced
2 teaspoons salt
½ cup white wine
Paprika

Shell and devein shrimp. Wash both shrimp and scallops. Place shrimp and scallops together in a large bowl. Combine lemon juice, olive oil, oregano, garlic, salt, and wine over shellfish and marinate at least 2 hours, or overnight in refrigerator, stirring occasionally. Pour in a large skillet and sprinkle with paprika. Cook over moderately low heat 10 to 15 minutes, or until fish is tender. Spoon into scallop shells, if available, or individual serving bowls.

Serves 12

Shrimp

S hrimp are in season year-round, and all shrimp, no matter what the variety, will turn pink when cooked.

Fresh shrimp can be sold by the pound and also by the size. Jumbo shrimp are usually the most expensive, but are easier to shell and devein. There's about 15 shrimp to a pound. Medium shrimp will run from 20 to 25 a pound, and the tiny shrimp will yield from 40 to 50 a pound. In general, you can serve six with about two pounds of unshelled shrimp, or one to one-and-a-half pounds of cooked and shelled shrimp.

The method of cleaning and shelling shrimp is relatively easy. Just snip the shell from head to tail along the back. Slip off the shell, and remove any grit by holding the shrimp under the faucet. Remove the black sand vein down the back. Rinse again and dry.

If you're using canned shrimp, try soaking them for an hour in lemon-squeezed ice water.

T he only thing to add to this dish of tasty morsels is more tasty morsels.

Lulu Brown's Boiled Shrimp

1	quart water	1	teaspoon salt
1	stalk celery	1½	pounds large shrimp
1	small onion, sliced	3	thin lemon slices
4	peppercorns	2	cups ketchup
1	bay leaf	½	cup horseradish

Combine water, celery, onion, peppercorns, bay leaf, and salt in saucepan. Bring to boil over moderately low heat, and allow to simmer while preparing shrimp. Shell and devein shrimp. Add shrimp and lemon slices to water.

Cover, bring to a boil and simmer 5 minutes until shrimp turn pink. Drain. Chill. For a zesty cocktail sauce, simply blend ketchup and horseradish together, and serve with chilled shrimp.

Serves 6

A perfect complement for this shrimp/mustard dip dish is a big bowl of cool Sesame Pasta Salad (p. 62) and a platter of fresh Asparagus Vinaigrette (p. 140). Wash it all down with a cool pitcher of mimosa punch . . . aaah!

Butterfry-Fly Shrimp

1 to 1½ pounds raw jumbo shrimp
Pepper
Garlic salt
6 tablespoons cornstarch
1 tablespoon dry sherry
1 tablespoon soy sauce
4 eggs, slightly beaten
½ cup flour
½ teaspoon baking powder
 Vegetable oil for frying
 Lemon wedges
 Mustard Dip (recipe follows)

Shell and devein shrimp and pat dry with paper towel. Split shrimp lengthwise almost through, being careful to leave the two halves joined. Sprinkle both sides of shrimp lightly with pepper and garlic salt. Dust shrimp lightly with cornstarch. In a bowl combine sherry and soy sauce. Add shrimp and stir to coat them. In another bowl, combine eggs, flour, and baking powder and stir until just smooth. Heat 3 inches of oil in a large skillet. Dip shrimp in egg batter and fry in heated oil about 3 or 4 minutes on each side, or until golden brown. Serve with lemon wedges and Mustard Dip.

Serves 4

Mustard Dip

2 tablespoons dry mustard
1 cup mayonnaise
¼ teaspoon Worcestershire sauce

In a small bowl combine mustard, mayonnaise, and Worcestershire sauce and blend well. Chill until served.

I have heard people say Shrimp Creole ain't "Creole" without okra . . . while that may be so, what do you do if you don't like okra?

Shrimp Creole

2 tablespoons olive oil	1/2 cup sliced celery
1 1/2 pounds raw medium-size shrimp, peeled and deveined	3/4 teaspoon cayenne pepper
1/2 cup thinly sliced onion	3/4 teaspoon garlic powder
8-ounce can tomato sauce	1 tablespoon chili powder
1 cup slivered green pepper	2 1/2 cups cooked rice

Heat oil in a large skillet over moderate heat. Add shrimp and cook until shrimp turns pink, stirring frequently. Remove with slotted spoon. To the same skillet, add onion and cook until lightly browned. Stir in tomato sauce, pepper, celery, cayenne, garlic powder, and chili powder. Simmer gently, uncovered, over moderately low heat 10 minutes. Add shrimp and heat thoroughly. Serve over cooked rice.

Serves 3 to 4

T o make this dish really authentic, wear suspenders and a belt.

Jambalaya

2 cups diced cooked ham	1/2 cup cooked fresh shrimp *or* 4 1/2 ounce can shrimp, drained
1 cup chopped green pepper	
1/2 cup chopped onion	1 medium bay leaf, crushed
1 garlic clove, minced	1/4 teaspoon crushed oregano
2 tablespoons butter *or* margarine	1/8 teaspoon salt
10 3/4 ounce can condensed tomato soup	Freshly ground pepper to taste
1/3 cup water	2 1/2 cups cooked rice

In 2-quart saucepan, place ham, green pepper, onion, garlic, and butter or margarine. Cook until the vegetables are tender. Stir in soup, water, shrimp, bay leaf, oregano, salt, and pepper. Cook over moderately low heat until sauce thickens. Bring sauce to a boil. Spoon over hot cooked rice.

Serves 4

*S*ome folks would go to the ends of the earth for a good smoke. I'd rather eat curry and live!

Shrimp Curry

3 pounds medium-size shrimp, peeled and deveined
3 tablespoons butter *or* margarine
1½ cup finely chopped onion
2 tablespoons curry powder
3 cans frozen cream of shrimp soup, thawed
⅓ cup milk

3 cups sour cream
5 cups cooked long-grain rice
Optional condiments:
Chopped cashew nuts
Chopped hard-cooked egg
Flaked coconut
Chutney

Cook shrimp in salted boiling water until shrimp turns pink. Peel and devein, then rinse under cold water. Melt butter in a large skillet or Dutch oven over moderately low heat. Add onion and curry powder, and cook, stirring frequently, until onion is tender. Remove from heat, and blend in soup and milk; add cooked shrimp. Return to heat and cook until hot, stirring constantly. Just before serving, fold in sour cream, and cook over low heat, stirring constantly, until thoroughly heated. Do not allow mixture to boil. Serve over hot rice. Serve the condiments on the side in small bowls to be sprinkled over each serving if desired.

Serves 8 to 10

*F*ortune cookie say: "Don't put all your kumquats in one basket."

Sweet & Sour Shrimp

2 pounds fresh shrimp in shell *or* 1 pound frozen, cleaned shrimp
8¼-ounce can sliced pineapple
1 medium-size green pepper, cut into strips
½ cup firmly packed brown sugar

¼ cup white vinegar
2 tablespoons soy sauce
1 cup water
3 tablespoons cornstarch
¼ cup water
3 cups cooked rice

Cook fresh shrimp in boiling salted water over moderate heat until shrimp turn pink. (Cook frozen shrimp following package directions.) Rinse in cold water and drain. If in the shell, clean and devein. Rinse in cold water and drain. Drain pineapple and reserve juice. Mix pineapple juice, green pepper, brown sugar, vinegar, soy sauce, and the 1 cup water in saucepan. Bring to a boil over moderately low heat 20 to 25 minutes, or until green pepper is almost tender. Blend cornstarch and the ¼ cup water together; stir into sauce. Cook, stirring constantly until thickened. Add shrimp and heat to serving temperature. Serve over rice. Garnish with pineapple slices.

Serves 6

*E*xcept for the avocado and tomato, this tangy appetizer may be prepared ahead. Serve it at brunch with Green & White Pasta Salad (p. 58) and a platter of sliced honeydew melon and strawberries sprinkled with Midori liqueur.

Avocado Shrimp Boats

12	ounces fresh *or* frozen shelled medium shrimp	1	small onion, thinly sliced
2	tablespoons white vinegar	1	clove garlic, halved
1½	teaspoons lemon juice	3	tablespoons cooking oil
¼	teaspoon salt	1	small pickled jalapeño pepper, rinsed, seeded, and cut in strips
⅛	teaspoon dry mustard	2	large avocados, halved and seeded
	Pepper to taste	1	medium tomato, chopped

Thaw frozen shrimp. In a bowl, combine vinegar, lemon juice, salt, mustard, and pepper; set aside. In a skillet, cook shrimp, half of the onion slices, and the garlic in hot oil over medium heat 4 to 5 minutes or until shrimp are done, stirring occasionally. Remove onion and garlic with slotted spoon; discard. Add shrimp and remaining oil to vinegar mixture in bowl, along with remaining sliced onion and the jalapeño pepper. Cover and chill several hours or overnight, stirring occasionally. To serve, lift shrimp, onion slices, and jalapeño peppers from marinade; spoon into avocado halves. Sprinkle with chopped tomato; drizzle some of the marinade over all.

Serves 4

"The cure for anything is salt water—
Sweat, tears or the sea."

Isak Dinesen

S*hould you choose to serve pasta with this colorful, art deco dish, make it either vermicelli or capellini (angel hair), which is even thinner than vermicelli. Add steamed, chilled broccoli spears vinaigrette, and for that final touch, choose a bottle of soave or Verdicchio.*

Shrimp with Artichokes

12 ounces fresh *or* frozen shelled shrimp	2 tablespoons dry sherry
9-ounce package frozen artichoke hearts *or* 14-ounce can artichoke hearts in water	1 tablespoon wine vinegar
7½-ounce can tomatoes, cut up	½ teaspoon dried basil, crushed
⅓ cup chopped green onion	½ teaspoon dried marjoram, crushed
2 tablespoons snipped parsley	½ teaspoon salt
2 tablespoons lemon juice	Pinch of pepper
	½ cup shredded fontina cheese
	¼ cup grated Parmesan cheese
	Hot cooked rice *or* pasta

In a saucepan, cook fresh or frozen shrimp in boiling, salted water until shrimp turns pink; drain. Cook frozen artichoke hearts according to package instructions; drain. (Or, drain canned artichoke hearts.)

In a large skillet, combine shrimp, artichoke hearts, *undrained* tomatoes, green onion, parsley, lemon juice, sherry, wine vinegar, basil, marjoram, salt, and pepper. Bring to a boil; reduce heat. Simmer, uncovered, about 10 minutes or till most of the liquid is evaporated. Sprinkle with cheese. Serve with hot rice or pasta.

Serves 4

Soups & Stews
The Basics

This section is made up of dishes which represent the mainstay of the meal, and all that's needed to complete the menu is warm, crusty bread and a tossed salad.

The variety of soups and stews is endless: beef, pork, lamb, poultry, fish, seafood, cheese, and vegetables.

Hearty soups are especially good in cold weather, and although they do take time to prepare, they may be made ahead and reheated at serving time. Most of these dishes will taste even better when the flavors have had a chance to marry.

Garnishes are often added to soups, not only for appearance's sake but because the garnish adds flavor to the dish.

You may wish to experiment with a dollop of sour cream, snipped parsley, watercress leaves, celery, croutons, onion, green pepper rings, or bacon crumbs as garnishes.

Dried herbs can lend a very interesting flavor (one at a time, of course) to certain soups. Try a pinch of dill with potato soup, basil with tomato soup, and tarragon with a creamed poultry soup. Also, for an additional warming feeling, pour a jigger of dry sherry into any cream soup; then just light the fire and enjoy!

"Of soup and love, the first is best."

Spanish Proverb

A most elegant beef stew which calls for a most elegant red wine! Try St. Emilion Burgundy or perhaps a St. Julien or Merlot.

Beef Bourguignonne

2	pounds beef stew meat, cut into 1-inch cubes	1	clove garlic, crushed
3	tablespoons all-purpose flour	1	bay leaf
3	tablespoons butter *or* margarine	½	teaspoon dried thyme, crushed
1	cup Burgundy	2	slices bacon, cut into small pieces
1	cup beef broth	1	pound small white onions
2	medium carrots, sliced	½	pound fresh mushrooms, sliced
2	stalks celery, sliced	2	tablespoons butter *or* margarine
1	tablespoon tomato paste	2	tablespoons snipped parsley
			Pepper

In a large bowl, toss the beef cubes with the flour. In a 4-quart Dutch oven, brown the beef cubes, half at a time, on all sides in the 3 tablespoons butter or margarine. Return all meat to pan. Add the Burgundy, beef broth, carrots, celery, tomato paste, garlic, bay leaf, and thyme. Cover and cook over moderate heat for 2 hours. In a skillet, cook and stir the bacon and small onions till bacon is crisp and onions are lightly browned; discard excess fat. Add to beef mixture and continue cooking, covered, 30 minutes more. In same skillet, cook the mushrooms in the 2 tablespoons butter or margarine 4 to 5 minutes or till tender. Just before serving, stir the mushrooms and parsley into the beef mixture. Season to taste with pepper.

Serves 8

D ry beans and dry whole peas need soaking before cooking, but split peas and lentils do not. Just rinse and drain these before cooking.

Bean & Burgundy Stew

2½	cups dry pinto beans	1	bay leaf
7	cups cold water	1	teaspoon salt
1	pound beef stew meat, cut into 1-inch cubes	½	teaspoon pepper
			16-ounce can tomatoes, cut up
7	cups hot water	1½	cups Burgundy
1	meaty ham hock		8-ounce can tomato sauce
1	clove garlic, minced	2	tablespoons packed brown sugar

In a Dutch oven, combine beans and the 7 cups cold water. Bring to boiling. Reduce heat and simmer, uncovered, 2 minutes. Remove from heat. Cover and let stand 1 hour (or, add beans to cold water; cover and let stand overnight). In a large saucepan, cook beef till browned. Drain and rinse soaked beans; add the 7 cups of hot water, the browned beef, ham hock, garlic, bay leaf, salt, and pepper. Bring to boiling. Cover; simmer 1½ hours, stirring occasionally. Remove meat from ham hock and return to stew. Add *undrained* tomatoes, Burgundy, tomato sauce, and brown sugar. Simmer, covered, about 45 minutes more or till beans are tender. Remove bay leaf. Season to taste with salt and pepper.

Serves 8

"Pleasantest of all ties is the tie of host and guest."

Aeschylus

*T*his French seafood/fish stew is in a category all its own; and as any gourmand will tell you, just taste it once, and you'll be hooked!

Bouillabaisse

2 6-ounce fresh *or* frozen lobster tails	¼ teaspoon fennel seed, crushed
2 pounds fresh or frozen fish filets, flounder *or* halibut *or* a combination of both	½ teaspoon salt
	¼ teaspoon pepper
	3 cups water
2 medium onions, chopped	1 cup dry white wine
4 ripe tomatoes, peeled and chopped	2 tablespoons tomato paste
2 tablespoons snipped parsley	1 dozen small clams in shells, scrubbed
2 cloves garlic, minced	
3 tablespoons olive oil	½ pound scallops, washed
1 teaspoon dried thyme, crushed	½ pound fresh shrimp, shelled and deveined, with tails left on
2 bay leaves	
¼ teaspoon saffron threads	

Cut membrane along both edges of each lobster tail and remove. Cut each tail into 3 or 4 pieces, leaving meat in shells. Cut fish into 1½-inch pieces.

In Dutch oven, cook onions, fresh tomatoes, parsley, and garlic in oil for 5 minutes, or till onion is tender. Add thyme, bay leaves, saffron, fennel, ½ teaspoon salt, and ¼ teaspoon pepper. Stir in 3 cups water, the wine, and tomato paste. Heat to boiling. Add fish, lobster, clams, scallops, and shrimp; return to a boil. Reduce heat and simmer, uncovered, 6 to 8 minutes, or till clams are opened and fish is done. Season to taste with additional salt and pepper. Discard bay leaves. Serve with sliced hot French bread.

Serves 8

T his recipe is very filling and is wonderful served for lunch. It will fortify you on those wintry days when Jack Frost is nipping at your nose.

Beefy-Barley Soup

2½ pounds beef stew meat, cut into 1-inch pieces	1 teaspoon dried thyme, crushed
1 clove garlic, minced	6 cups water
1 tablespoon vegetable oil	1½ teaspoon salt
8-ounce can tomatoes, cut up	½ teaspoon pepper
8-ounce can tomato sauce	1½ cups sliced carrots
1 cup dry red wine	1 stalk celery, sliced
1 bay leaf	½ cup pearl barley
	¼ cup snipped parsley

In a Dutch oven, cook beef and garlic in hot oil till beef is browned; drain. Stir in *undrained* tomatoes, tomato sauce, wine, bay leaf, thyme, 6 cups water, 1½ teaspoon salt, and ½ teaspoon pepper. Bring to boiling; reduce heat. Simmer, covered, for 1 hour. Stir in carrots, celery, and barley. Simmer, uncovered, 1 hour more, stirring occasionally. Remove bay leaf. Skim off any fat. Stir in parsley.

Serves 6 to 8

S it your friends down for a leisurely appetizer of French-Dip Artichokes (p. 151), to be followed by this curried soup, and perhaps a platter of pita bread and assorted cheeses.

Curried Chicken Soup

1 medium apple, peeled and chopped	1 cup cooked rice
1 medium onion, chopped	½ cup golden raisins
4 teaspoons curry powder	¼ teaspoon salt
¼ cup butter *or* margarine	Pinch white pepper
4 cups chicken broth	½ cup sour cream
2 cups cubed cooked chicken	¼ cup coarsely chopped peanuts

In a large saucepan, cook the apple, onion, and curry powder in the butter or margarine till the onion is tender. Stir in the broth, chicken, rice, raisins, salt, and pepper. Bring to a boil. Reduce heat. Cover and simmer 15 minutes. Gradually blend about 1 cup of the hot mixture into sour cream. Return all to saucepan and stir to combine thoroughly. Stir in peanuts.

Serves 4

M ake this fine stew any time of the year, and I promise, you'll find yourself walking along some distant shoreline with the taste of salt on your lips!

Cape Cod Stew

1	pound fresh white fish (cod, haddock, *or* sole)		Pinch pepper
1	small onion, diced	1	bay leaf
1	clove garlic, minced	2	cups potatoes, peeled and sliced
2	tablespoons butter *or* margarine	½	cup sliced carrots
1	cup water	2	medium tomatoes, peeled and chopped
½	cup dry vermouth	6	fresh mushrooms, sliced
1	chicken bouillon cube	2	tablespoons snipped parsley
1	teaspoon salt	½	cup cold water
½	teaspoon dried marjoram	2	tablespoons cornstarch

Cut fish into bite-size pieces. In a large saucepan or Dutch oven, cook onion and garlic in butter or margarine till tender, but not brown. Stir in the cup of water and add the following 8 listed ingredients. Bring to a boil. Reduce heat; cover and simmer about 20 minutes or till vegetables are tender. Add fish, tomatoes, mushrooms, and parsley. Cover and simmer about 5 minutes or till fish flakes easily with a fork. Remove fish; set aside. Combine ½ cup cold water and cornstarch; stir into saucepan. Cook and stir till thickened and bubbly. Cook and stir 1 to 2 minutes more. Return fish to saucepan; heat through.

Serves 4

"After a good dinner, one can forgive anybody, even one's own relations."

Oscar Wilde

*I*f you're serving this soup as the center of the meal, that's fine. However, if you're serving it as a first course, I'd suggest you follow it with a Pasta Chicken-Curry Salad (p. 61) and a chilled bottle of Gewürztraminer.

Corny Chicken Soup

½ cup chopped onion	2½ cups milk
¼ cup chopped celery	14½-ounce can chicken broth *or*
1 clove garlic, minced	2 cups homemade broth
3 tablespoons butter *or* margarine	1½ cups cubed cooked chicken
3 tablespoons all-purpose flour	12-ounce can whole kernel corn
½ teaspoon salt	with sweet peppers
¼ teaspoon dried marjoram	1 cup cooked rice
¼ teaspoon dried thyme	

In a saucepan, cook onion, celery, and garlic in butter or margarine till vegetables are tender. Stir flour, salt, marjoram, and thyme into vegetable mixture, blending well. Stir in milk and broth. Cook and stir till slightly thickened and bubbly. Cook 1 to 2 minutes more. Stir in chicken, *undrained* corn, and rice. Continue cooking 5 to 10 minutes more or till heated through.

Serves 4 to 6

*F*or such a rich, creamy soup, simply place warmed slices of buttered sourdough bread in a basket, along with a tossed green salad topped with ranch dressing.

Creamy Zucchini Chicken Soup

½ cup water	2 tablespoons butter *or* margarine
2 cups shredded zucchini	2 tablespoons all-purpose flour
½ cup shredded carrot	¼ teaspoon salt
½ cup chopped celery	¼ teaspoon white pepper
½ cup chopped onion	1½ cups milk
2 tablespoons snipped parsley	½ cup light cream *or* half and half
1 pinch seasoned salt	2 cups finely chopped cooked chicken
1 chicken bouillon cube	

In a medium saucepan combine water, zucchini, carrot, celery, onion, parsley, seasoned salt, and bouillon cube. Cook about 5 minutes or until zucchini is tender. Place half of the *undrained* zucchini mixture in blender or food processor; cover and blend till smooth. Set aside. Repeat with remaining zucchini.

Melt butter or margarine in saucepan, stir in flour, salt and pepper. Stir in milk and light cream. Cook and stir till thickened and bubbly. Stir in chicken and zucchini mixture. Cook and stir 5 minutes more or till heated through.

Serves 4

*P**ractically everything but the kitchen sink goes into this pot, and it may take a knife, a fork, and a spoon to eat it.*

Hearty Chicken Stew

	2½- to 3-pound broiler-fryer chicken, cut up	1	large onion, sliced
4	cups water	½	cup chopped green pepper
1	teaspoon salt	2	tablespoons Worcestershire sauce
½	teaspoon celery salt	1	teaspoon sugar
1	bay leaf	½	teaspoon cayenne pepper
	16-ounce can stewed tomatoes	½	teaspoon ground cumin
6	carrots, chunky cut	½	teaspoon ground ginger
6	new potatoes (red-skin), cut in quarters	½	cup cold water
		¼	cup all-purpose flour

Place chicken in 5-quart Dutch oven or large stew pot. Add water, salt, celery salt, and bay leaf. Bring to a boil. Reduce heat; cover and simmer about 1 hour or until chicken is tender. Remove chicken from broth. Skim off fat, and reserve 3 cups of broth; reserve remainder for another recipe. When chicken is cool enough to handle, remove skin and bones from chicken; discard skin and bones. Cut up chicken and set aside. Meanwhile, in Dutch oven, combine reserved broth, *undrained* stewed tomatoes, carrots, potatoes, onion, green pepper, Worcestershire sauce, sugar, ground cayenne pepper, cumin, and ginger. Bring to a boil; reduce heat. Cover and let cool until the vegetables are fork-tender. Combine water and flour; stir till smooth. Stir into stew along with chicken. Cook and stir till thickened and bubbly. Remove bay leaf.

Serves 6

"Poetry is the only art people haven't learned yet to consume like soup."
W. H. Auden

*H*ave this pot of stew simmering off the top of your stove when your hunter comes through the door as hungry as a bear, and watch what happens!

Hunter's Stew

1	pound Polish sausage (kielbasa), sliced diagonally in 1-inch pieces	1	medium onion, chopped
1/4	pound fresh mushrooms, sliced	1	bay leaf
1	large apple, peeled, cored, and chopped	5	peppercorns
	27-ounce jar sauerkraut, drained	1	clove garlic, minced
			16-ounce can tomatoes, cut up
		6	strips cooked bacon, crumbled

In a Dutch oven, layer 1/2 of each of the following in the order listed: sausage, mushrooms, apple, sauerkraut, onion, bay leaf, peppercorns, garlic, and tomatoes. Sprinkle with bacon. Repeat layers. Cover and cook on medium heat for two hours. Remove bay leaf and peppercorns.

Serves 4

"An army marches on its stomach!"

Napoleon Bonaparte

*B*read plates, piled high with pumpernickel and sweet butter, and goblets of Burgundy, make this ragout "the specialty of the house"!

Lamb Ragout

1 1/2	pounds boneless lamb, cut into 1-inch pieces	1/2	teaspoon mint flakes, crushed
1	clove garlic, minced	1/4	teaspoon dried rosemary
2	tablespoons cooking oil	3	medium new potatoes, peeled and quartered
2 1/4	cups water	6	whole small carrots
1	medium onion, sliced	2	tablespoons butter *or* margarine, melted
1	bay leaf		
1	beef bouillon cube	2	tablespoons all-purpose flour
1	teaspoon celery salt		

In a Dutch oven, cook lamb and garlic in hot oil till meat is browned. Drain off fat. Add water, together with the following six listed ingredients. Bring to a boil; reduce heat. Cover and simmer for 30 minutes. Add potatoes and carrots.

Cover and continue cooking about 30 minutes or till lamb and vegetables are tender. Remove bay leaf. In a small bowl, combine melted butter or margarine and flour, blending till smooth. Stir flour mixture into ragout, mixing well. Cook and stir till thickened and bubbly.

Serves 6

"Blessed are the brief, for they will be invited again."

Anonymous

T his lamb stew is a trifle bland in its seasoning, but, when I think of Irish wit and poetry, and those challenging blue eyes, it's the only thing Irish I know of that is bland.

Maggie's Irish Lamb Stew

1 pound boneless lamb, cut into 1-inch cubes	2 carrots, sliced
1 medium onion, cut into thin wedges	1 medium turnip, peeled and chopped
1½ teaspoons salt	1 tablespoon snipped parsley
¼ teaspoon pepper	¼ teaspoon dried thyme, crushed
3½ cups water	2 to 3 tablespoons flour
3 new potatoes, peeled and sliced	½ cup cold water
	Salt and pepper

In a Dutch oven, combine the lamb, onion, salt and pepper, and 3½ cups of water. Bring to a boil. Reduce heat; cover and simmer 40 minutes. Stir in potatoes, carrots, turnip, parsley, and thyme. Cover; cook 20 minutes more or till vegetables are tender. Combine flour and ½ cup cold water. Add to meat vegetable mixture. Cook and stir till thickened and bubbly. Cook and stir 1 minute more. Season with salt and pepper.

Serves 4

*W*hen I was visiting Nice in the south of France, I found a tiny restaurant sitting on the shore of the Mediterranean. A woman wearing an apron emerged from the kitchen carrying bowls of this soup. Her recipe, however, was to remain her secret, so I created my own.

French Chowder

1	cup dry pinto beans			8-ounce can tomato sauce
5	cups cold water		¾	cup red wine
5	cups hot water		½	cup chopped onion
10	breakfast sausage links, cooked and drained		½	teaspoon garlic powder
			½	teaspoon dried thyme, crushed
2	cups fully cooked ham, cubed		1	bay leaf
2	cups cooked chicken, cubed			Salt and pepper
1½	cups sliced carrots			

In a large saucepan or Dutch oven, combine beans with the 5 cups cold water. Bring to a boil. Reduce heat; cover and simmer for 1½ hours. Drain; stir in the 5 cups of hot water, the sausage links, ham, chicken, carrots, tomato sauce, wine, onion, garlic powder, thyme, and bay leaf. Bring to a boil; reduce heat. Cover and simmer about 45 minutes more. Remove bay leaf. Season the chowder to taste with salt and pepper.

Serves 8 to 10

*O*f all the colonies, those of New England shall always remain the brightest in my memory. Winter, summer, spring, and fall: the four seasons, so taken for granted, and so sorely missed. But, joyfully, with one bowl of this creamy chowder shared with life-long friends, I smile, knowing I am where I want to be.

New England Clam Chowder

¼	cup finely chopped salt pork		2	cups milk
1	medium onion, finely chopped		1	cup light cream
2	cups diced potatoes		1	tablespoon flour
1	teaspoon salt		2	tablespoons milk
½	teaspoon pepper		2	tablespoons dry sherry
2	6½-ounce cans minced clams *or* 1 quart shucked fresh clams, diced			

Cook salt pork in a heavy saucepan over moderate heat until crisp and brown. Drain crisp pieces on paper towels. Cook onion in the fat until tender. Add diced potatoes, salt and pepper, and liquid drained from the clams. Add water, if necessary, to cover the potatoes; cook over moderately low heat until potatoes are tender. Add clams. Stir in the 2 cups of milk and cream and set aside to ripen for a couple of hours. Reheat slowly over very low heat. Stir flour and the 2 tablespoons of milk together to form a smooth paste. Stir into chowder, and cook slowly over moderately low heat, stirring constantly, until slightly thickened. The chowder will be more flavorful if you can allow it to stand in the refrigerator for 24 hours. Reheat over very low heat, adding the sherry. Serve with crackers.

Serves 4 to 6

> *"Things are seldom what they seem,*
> *Skim milk masquerades as cream."*
>
> W. S. Gilbert

*T*urn *your kitchen into a sea shanty for four, starting with either Avocado Shrimp Boats (p. 113) or By The Sea-Shell Salad (p. 57), followed with steaming bowls of clam chowder and Lobster Tails in Butter Sauce (p. 103). Believe me, King Neptune never had it so good.*

Manhattan Clam Chowder

2	6½-ounce cans minced clams *or* 1 quart shucked fresh clams, diced	1	medium-size green pepper, chopped
½	cup finely diced salt pork	1	bay leaf
1	large onion, coarsely chopped	½	teaspoon dried thyme
1	medium-size leek, sliced	5	cups water
2	medium-size potatoes, peeled and cubed	2	teaspoons salt
4	large tomatoes, peeled and chopped	½	teaspoon pepper
1	celery stalk, chopped	½	teaspoon caraway seeds

Drain clams and reserve both clams and liquid. Place salt pork in a large Dutch oven. Cook over moderately low heat about 2 minutes. Add onion and leek and cook until tender. Add the following 7 listed ingredients plus the liquid from clams. Add salt and pepper and blend well. Bring to a boil over moderate heat, then simmer, covered, over moderately low heat for 30 to 35 minutes, or until vegetables are tender. Add minced clams and caraway seeds. Cook 5 minutes.

Serves 4

T his meal-in-one soup is an excellent use for leftover turkey, especially around Thanksgiving.

Thanksgiving Stew

1	turkey carcass		2	large sweet potatoes, split length-
4	cups water			wise and cut
2	cans (10½-ounces each) cream of		1	tablespoon Worcestershire sauce
	chicken soup		½	teaspoon garlic powder
	16-ounce can stewed tomatoes		¼	teaspoon dried oregano, crushed
2	cups sliced carrots		¼	teaspoon dried basil, crushed
½	pound green beans, cut		½	teaspoon black pepper
2	cups chopped celery		3	cups cubed cooked turkey
1	medium onion, chopped		½	pound sliced mushrooms

In a stockpot or Dutch oven combine turkey carcass with water and cream of chicken soup, then stir gently. Add *undrained* stewed tomatoes, carrots, green beans, celery, onion, sweet potatoes, Worcestershire sauce, garlic powder, oregano, basil, and ½ teaspoon of black pepper. Bring to boiling; reduce heat. Cover and simmer until potatoes are fork-tender, stirring occasionally. Add turkey and mushrooms. Bring to boil. Reduce heat. Cover; simmer 10 minutes more.

Serves 6

I t *just doesn't get any better than this!*

Old-Fashioned Beef Stew

½ cup all-purpose flour	1 bay leaf
½ teaspoon salt	1 teaspoon dried thyme, crushed
¼ teaspoon pepper	½ teaspoon salt
1½ pounds beef stew meat, cut into 1-inch cubes	6 new potatoes, peeled
3 tablespoons cooking oil	3 medium carrots, cut into ½-inch pieces
2 cups beef broth	1 medium onion, chopped
1 cup dry red wine	½ pound cut green beans
3 tablespoons tomato paste	8½-ounce can small peas
1 clove garlic, minced	

In a large bowl or plastic bag, combine flour, ½ teaspoon salt, and ¼ teaspoon pepper. Add meat cubes, a few at a time, coating completely. In a Dutch oven, brown meat on all sides in hot oil. Drain off excess fat. Stir in beef broth, wine, tomato paste, garlic, bay leaf, thyme, and ½ teaspoon salt. Cover and simmer 1 hour. Add potatoes, carrots, and onion; simmer 15 minutes more. Stir in green beans and peas; simmer 15 minutes more or till meat and vegetables are tender. Remove bay leaf. Season to taste.

Serves 6

T his delicate, creamy soup is wonderful when followed by Fish Filets and *Asparagus Roll-ups (p. 87) accompanied by Sunny Risotto Lemonese (p. 80). A lovely, light rosé Anjou or Chardonnay completes the meal.*

Shrimp Bisque

2 tablespoons butter *or* margarine	1 cup light cream
1 medium onion, sliced into rings	1 cup milk
3 tablespoons all-purpose flour	½ pound small cooked shrimp
½ teaspoon pepper	½ cup shredded Swiss cheese
14½-ounce can chicken broth	Optional: croutons

In large saucepan, melt butter or margarine; add onion and cook till onion is tender. Stir in flour and pepper. Gradually stir in chicken broth, light cream, and milk. Cook and stir over medium heat till thickened. Stir in shrimp and cheese. Continue cooking and stirring till cheese is melted. Place the croutons, if desired, at the bottom of each serving bowl, and ladle soup over.

Serves 4

T his very special dish may be prepared with either sweet Italian sausage or sliced cooked chicken. Either way, your family and friends will enjoy it and ask you again and again, "When's tortellini night?"

Tortellini Soup Especial

6	cups water	1	small green bell pepper, cored and diced
1	pound sweet Italian sausage		
4	14½-ounce cans beef broth (if cooking with sausage) *or*	2	medium zucchini, sliced
	3 cups cooked chicken	1	small red onion, chopped
		1	medium tomato, diced
4	14½-ounce cans chicken broth (if cooking with chicken)	1	teaspoon chopped fresh basil
			Salt and freshly ground pepper
2	9-ounce boxes tortellini		Optional: freshly grated Parmesan cheese
½	pound spinach, shredded		

Combine all the ingredients in a large pot. If cooking with sausage, cut sausage into ½-inch pieces, and cook in saucepan until well-browned. Bring to slow boil over medium-high heat. Add salt and pepper. Reduce heat and simmer for about 15 minutes until the vegetables are tender. Serve promptly, passing the grated Parmesan cheese.

Makes 4 quarts

W hen using cheese in soups and stews or anything else, remember that when the cheese is melted, it is cooked. Do not continue to cook it, as it will become stringy. Cheese that is shredded or cut into small pieces melts best.

Vegetable/Cheese Soup

1	cup dry navy beans	2	cups coarsely chopped cabbage
8	cups cold water	1	medium zucchini, sliced
8	cups hot water	1	teaspoon dried basil
	15-ounce can tomato sauce	1	teaspoon dried oregano
1	cup chopped carrots	½	teaspoon dried thyme
1	medium onion, chopped	½	cup elbow macaroni
2	cloves garlic, minced	2	cups cubed Monterey Jack cheese
1	beef bouillon cube		

In a large sauce pan or Dutch oven, combine beans and cold water. Bring to a boil; reduce heat and simmer 2 minutes. Remove from heat. Cover; let stand 1 hour. (Or, soak beans in the water overnight in a covered pan.) Drain and rinse soaked beans; add the 8 cups of hot water. Bring to a boil. Reduce heat. Cover and simmer 2 hours. Add following 5 listed ingredients, then cover and simmer for 30 minutes. Add cabbage, zucchini, basil, oregano, and thyme to soup. Bring to a boil; stir in macaroni. Reduce heat; simmer, uncovered, for 10 to 15 minutes or just till macaroni is tender. When ladled out, sprinkle each serving with cubes of Monterey Jack cheese.

Serves 6

F or some unknown reason, whenever I'm preparing this hearty meal-in-one, I envision hordes of Mongolian troops encamped around my house, waiting for me to shout, "Dinner's ready!" Then the door flies open, and it's only Sidney and Sasha, my neighbor's twin sheepdogs. Back to reality!

Veal and Lentil Soup

2	pounds veal shanks	1/2	teaspoon dried rosemary, crushed
2	tablespoons vegetable oil	7	cups water
1	medium onion, chopped	1/2	teaspoon salt
1/2	cup snipped parsley	1/4	teaspoon pepper
1	chicken bouillon cube	1 1/2	cups dry lentils
1/2	teaspoon celery salt	3	medium carrots, sliced
1	teaspoon dried basil, crushed		

In a Dutch oven, brown shanks in hot oil; drain. Add onion, parsley, bouillon cube, celery salt, basil, rosemary, 7 cups water, 1/2 teaspoon salt, and 1/4 teaspoon pepper. Bring to a boil; reduce heat. Cover and simmer 30 minutes. Add lentils and carrots; simmer 45 minutes. Remove shanks. When cool to the touch, remove meat from bones. Cut up meat and return to soup. Discard bones. Heat meat through.

Serves 6

"He is a sorry cook, that may not lick his own finger."

John Ray

Veal
The Basics

Veal is the meat of a very young calf. It is delicate and expensive.

"Scaloppine" is simply a veal cutlet cut very thin and pounded flat. Veal cutlets should be cooked "off the top of your stove," because the meat is already dry, and broiling only makes it drier.

One of the most overlooked and seldom cooked of the veal cuts is the veal shank. It is one of the least expensive and is the main ingredient in Osso Buco. I promise you it is a slice of "La Dolce Vita"!

"Take thine ease,
Eat, drink and be merry."

Luke 7:9

A *pleasing partnership with the veal chops is a platter of Vermicelli with Mushrooms & Prosciutto (p. 56) and Asparagus Vinaigrette (p. 140).*

Stove-Top Veal Chops

	3 to 5 tablespoons butter *or* margarine	1	teaspoon salt
4	thick shoulder veal chops	¼	teaspoon pepper
	10½-ounce can tomato puree	½	cup finely chopped fresh parsley
1	cup dry white wine	2	to 3 cloves garlic, crushed
		1	tablespoon grated lemon peel

Heat 3 tablespoons butter or margarine in large skillet over moderate heat; add meat and increase heat to moderately high; cook until lightly browned (add more butter or margarine as needed). Mix tomato puree, wine, salt, and pepper, and pour over meat. Cover and simmer over low heat for 1 hour and 15 minutes, or until fork-tender. Combine parsley, garlic, and lemon peel; spoon over chops. Cover and simmer 10 minutes longer.

Serves 4

"**M**arinara" sounds like it should be a little girl's name . . . maybe it is, somewhere.

Veal Cutlets Marinara

½ cup seasoned bread crumbs
¼ cup grated Parmesan cheese
4 teaspoons paprika

1¼ pounds veal cutlet, pounded thin
    and cut into 4 pieces
3 tablespoons butter *or* margarine

Combine bread crumbs, grated cheese, and paprika in a bowl; mix thoroughly. Coat veal cutlets lightly with the bread crumb mixture. Melt butter or margarine in a large skillet over moderately low heat. Add cutlets, brown 4 to 5 minutes on each side, until meat is fork-tender. Serve immediately with the Marinara sauce.

Marinara Sauce

  16-ounce can tomatoes, diced
2 tablespoons olive oil
1 tablespoon water
1 tablespoon dried parsley flakes
1¼ teaspoons dried basil leaves,
    crushed

½ teaspoon sugar
2 teaspoons salt
3 whole peppercorns
  Dash of cayenne pepper

(Note: Marinara sauce should be prepared before the veal). Combine all ingredients in a Dutch oven, and over moderate heat, cook for 20 to 30 minutes, until sauce is blended and slightly thickened, stirring occasionally. Spoon over veal cutlets.

Serves 4

*T*his is a very rich dish, so the vegetable and salad should be kept simple. Steamed asparagus with a pat of butter and a squeeze of lemon, and a mixed green salad starring sliced mushrooms only.

Cheesy Veal Scallops

1	pound veal leg sirloin steak, cut ¼-inch thick	4	tablespoons butter *or* margarine
	Salt and pepper	1	teaspoon brandy
½	pound bacon	1	small chopped onion
3½	ounces Brie *or* Croustin cheese cut in 2-inch strips	1	cup whipping cream
		12	ounces cooked noodles

Cut veal into 4 pieces; pound with meat mallet to ⅛ thickness. Sprinkle with salt and pepper. Cook bacon, and cut into 1½-inch pieces. Put several strips of cheese and bacon in the center of each veal scallop. Roll and secure with string. Saute the veal rolls in butter or margarine. When browned on all sides, flame with brandy. Cover and simmer for 15 minutes, adding the onion after 7 minutes of cooking time. Remove veal scallops from pan, remove string, and arrange rolls on serving platter. Add whipping cream to cooking liquid in pan. Simmer until thickened. Pour sauce over veal and serve immediately with hot cooked noodles.

Serves 4

*"It's good food and not fine words
That keep me alive."*
Molière

*I*nstead of plain rice, try the Razzle-Dazzle Risotto (p. 81) and individual bowls of beet salad.

Georgian-Style Veal

1½	pounds boneless veal, cut in 1-inch pieces	¼	teaspoon dried oregano, crushed
½	cup water	¼	cup chopped onion
¼	cup chopped onion	¼	cup chopped pecans
1	chicken bouillon cube	1	tablespoon butter *or* margarine
1	clove garlic, minced	3	tablespoons flour
½	teaspoon salt	½	cup sour cream
¼	teaspoon dried thyme, crushed		Hot cooked rice

In a 3-quart saucepan or Dutch oven, combine veal, water, ¼ cup onion, bouillon cube, garlic, salt, thyme, and oregano. Simmer, uncovered, about 45 to 60 minutes or till meat is tender. Drain meat, reserving broth. Measure broth and add water, if needed, to make 1½ cups. In a small saucepan, cook ¼ cup onion and chopped pecans in butter or margarine till onion is tender, but not brown. Remove saucepan from heat. Blend flour into sour cream; stir in reserved broth mixture. Add to veal along with pecan mixture; mix well. Return to heat. Cook and stir till sauce is thickened and meat is heated through. Serve with hot cooked rice, if desired.

Serves 6

S *tart the first part of the meal with Clams & White Wine Broth (p. 94), and to accompany the veal, Spaghetti with Garlic & Olive Oil (p. 55) and a serving bowl of Chilled Herbed Mushrooms (p. 146).*

Stuffed Veal Rolls

1	whole medium chicken breast	8	ounces mozzarella cheese, sliced
1	cup water	1	medium tomato, peeled, seeded,
1	beaten egg		and chopped
¼	teaspoon dried tarragon, crushed	⅓	cup fine dry bread crumbs
¼	teaspoon salt	2	tablespoons grated Parmesan cheese
1½	pounds veal leg sirloin steak, cut	2	tablespoons snipped parsley
	¼-inch thick	¼	cup butter *or* margarine, melted
	Salt and pepper		Vegetable oil

In a small saucepan, combine chicken and 1 cup water. Cover and simmer about 20 minutes or till tender. Remove chicken; cool slightly. Discard skin and bones. Chop chicken; blend in beaten egg, tarragon, and ¼ teaspoon salt. Cut veal into 6 pieces; pound with meat mallet to about ⅛-inch thickness. Sprinkle with salt and pepper. Place cheese on each piece of veal, cutting to fit within ½-inch of edges. Spread each with chicken mixture. Top with tomato and, folding in sides, roll up jelly-roll style, pressing to seal well. Combine bread crumbs, Parmesan cheese, and parsley. Dip veal in melted butter or margarine, then roll in crumb mixture. Add vegetable oil to 10-inch skillet, and heat over moderate heat. Add veal rolls, and simmer, covered about 45 to 55 minutes, turning occasionally.

Serves 6

*O**sso Buco literally means "hollow bone," and is traditionally served with Risotto Milanese (p. 80). It's beautifully accompanied by a fresh spinach salad topped with marinated artichoke hearts and sliced mushrooms.*

Osso Buco

3	whole veal shanks, sawed into 2½-inch pieces	1	clove garlic, minced
	Salt and pepper		28-ounce can tomatoes, cut up
3	tablespoons flour	1	cup dry white wine
¼	cup vegetable oil	1	bay leaf
1	cup chopped onion	1	beef bouillon cube
½	cup chopped carrot	½	teaspoon dried thyme, crushed
½	cup chopped celery	1	cup water
			Salt and pepper

Sprinkle meat with salt and pepper. Coat lightly with flour, shaking off excess. In Dutch oven, slowly brown meat in hot cooking oil; remove meat. Add onion, carrot, celery, and garlic; cook till onion and celery are tender. Drain off fat. Return meat to Dutch oven. Stir in *undrained* tomatoes, wine, bay leaf, bouillon cube, dried thyme, 1 cup water, and salt and pepper. Bring to a boil, and reduce heat. Cover and simmer 1½ hours or until meat is fork-tender, stirring occasionally.

Serves 6

*O**n the same plate, add a serving of Pasta with Green Onions & Vermouth (p. 52), with a simple salad of romaine and iceberg lettuce topped with slices of hearts of palm and your favorite dressing.*

Veal Parmigiana

1½	pounds thin veal cutlets	8	ounces mozzarella cheese, thinly sliced
1	egg slightly beaten		Grated Parmesan cheese
¾	cup seasoned bread crumbs		
¼	cup butter *or* margarine		
	16-ounce jar meatless spaghetti sauce		

Dip veal cutlets in egg and then coat well with bread crumbs. Heat butter or margarine in skillet over moderately low heat, add veal and increase temperature to moderately high; cook veal until well browned on both sides. Pour a layer of spaghetti sauce into the bottom of a shallow, 2½-quart heavy skillet, and then arrange the veal in a single layer over sauce. Arrange the sliced mozzarella cheese over veal and cover tightly. Cook over very low heat until mozzarella cheese is melted thoroughly (about 10 minutes). Serve with grated Parmesan cheese, if desired.

Serves 4

"I saw him even now going the way of all flesh, that is to say towards the kitchen."

John Webster

T *his dish should be served immediately. It's exceptional spooned over a serving of fresh, hot, cooked linguine, with a crunchy loaf of French bread and a bottle of Beaujolais.*

Veal & Green Peppers

3 medium-size green peppers	2 cups canned whole, peeled tomatoes
2 tablespoons vegetable oil	
1 large onion, sliced	1 teaspoon salt
1 pound veal shoulder, cut into 1-inch cubes	Few grains pepper
	⅓ cup dry white wine

Wash, stem, and seed green peppers; cut each into six sections. Heat 1 tablespoon vegetable oil in skillet over moderately low heat; add onion and green pepper and cook until tender, stirring frequently. Remove onions and green pepper. Add the remaining 1 tablespoon oil to the skillet and heat; add veal and cook over moderately high heat until lightly browned, stirring occasionally. Add tomatoes, salt, and pepper; cover and cook over low heat for 30 minutes. Return green pepper and onion and add wine to pan and cook 30 minutes longer.

Serves 4

F or a delicious combination, you can serve either Pasta with Butter & Cream (p. 50) or Risotto & Mushrooms (p. 82), Sautéed Zucchini (p. 158), and individual lettuce-lined bowls of Marinated Cherry Tomatoes (p. 155).

Veal Piccata

Salt
1½ pounds veal cutlet, pounded very
    thin and cut into 12 pieces
Flour
4   tablespoons butter *or* margarine

¼ cup lemon juice
¼ cup dry white wine
2   tablespoons finely chopped parsley
    Lemon slices

Sprinkle salt lightly on both sides of the veal. Coat veal pieces with flour and shake off any excess. Melt 2 tablespoons of the butter or margarine in a large skillet over moderately high heat. Add veal pieces and brown about 4 minutes on each side. Add the remaining 2 tablespoons of butter as needed during browning. Reduce heat to moderately low; add lemon juice, wine, and parsley. Cook for about 8 minutes. Garnish with lemon slices, and additional chopped parsley, if desired.

Serves 4 to 6

T onight, as the Italians often do, you can enjoy a first course of Vermicelli with Mushrooms & Prosciutto (p. 56). With Veal Marsala, serve the Rata- touille (p. 157) with freshly grated Parmesan cheese.

Veal Scaloppine Marsala

½ teaspoon garlic salt
¼ cup flour
    Few grains pepper
    Dash ground nutmeg

1½ pounds veal for scaloppine
¼ cup butter *or* margarine
½ cup Marsala

Mix together garlic salt, flour, pepper, and nutmeg. Coat veal slices with this mixture. Melt butter in a large skillet over moderately high heat and sauté veal until lightly browned on both sides, a total of 5 minutes. Remove from heat. Place veal slices on a platter and keep warm.

Stir the Marsala into the skillet, loosening the browned bits on the bottom of the pan. Heat to serving temperature, and pour over veal.

Serves 4

Vegetables
The Basics

"**E**at your vegetables" is every mother's plaintive cry to children around the world. Vegetables that taste good will encourage anyone to eat them—even more than the idea that they're good for you.

The best way to ensure their flavor is not to overcook them. When preparing, bear in mind that the idea is to *preserve* the original flavor, not *mask* it.

Following are a few basic ways to prepare vegetables:

To steam   This is a good way to cook them, because when done properly, they retain the most nutrients and flavor. You'll need a large pot with a steamer basket to hold the vegetables about ½ inch or so above the boiling water. Bring the water to a boil, place them in the steamer basket, and cook to preferred doneness—usually just a few minutes.

To braise   Put vegetables in a skillet with a little fat and a small amount of water and salt. Add vegetables such as sliced carrots, zucchini, asparagus, endive, young green beans, and summer squash. Cover tightly and cook until vegetables are just tender.

To boil   Except for some root vegetables, it only takes ½ to 1 cup of water to cook six servings of tender, fresh vegetables.

To pan fry   Heat 2 or 3 tablespoons of butter or margarine in a heavy skillet over medium heat. Fry cooked sliced potatoes or sweet potatoes or carrots until golden. Dip slices of eggplant, summer squash, and zucchini into seasoned flour and cook until tender and browned.

To french fry   French frying is a method of cooking food in enough hot melted shortening to cover the food being fried. Potatoes, eggplant sticks, and onion rings are all good when french fried. Most vegetables, except potatoes, will fry best if they are dipped in a batter.

Vegetables, remember, are a nutritional necessity—they are a main source of Vitamins A and C. They're especially appealing to the weight-conscious. Raw vegetables are a boon to anyone watching his weight, and even teenagers have been known to indulge.

Have you ever wondered when certain vegetables are at their peak? Well, wonder no more! Let the following seasonal buying chart be your guide . . .

Vegetable	Season
Artichokes, globe	March-May
Asparagus	April, May
Beets	June-October
Broccoli	October-April
Brussels sprouts	September-February
Cauliflower	October
Corn	May-September
Endive, Belgian	October-May
Leeks	October-May
Okra	June-August
Peas	May-September
Sweet potatoes	September-December
Tomatoes	May-August

"What has grown from the earth goes back to the earth, but what has sprung from heavenly seed, back to the heavenly realms returns."
Euripides

Cooking Fresh Vegetables

Cook the vegetables in a covered pan of boiling salted water, until just tender. Just follow the chart for perfectly cooked vegetables.

Vegetable	Cooking Time
Artichokes	20 to 30 min.
Asparagus (whole)	10 to 15 min.
Asparagus (cut-up)	8 to 10 min.
Beans (whole or cut up)	20 to 30 min.
Beets (whole)	35 to 50 min.
Beets (cut up)	15 to 20 min.
Broccoli (cut in spears)	10 to 15 min.
(for salad)	8 to 10 min.
Brussels sprouts	10 to 15 min.
Cabbage (cut in wedges)	10 to 12 min.
Cabbage (shredded)	5 to 7 min.
Carrots (cut up)	10 to 20 min.
Cauliflower (whole)	About 20 min.
(cut in flowerets)	10 to 15 min.
Celery (sliced)	10 to 15 min.
Corn (ears)	6 to 8 min.
(cut off cobs)	12 to 15 min.
Eggplant (sliced)	Cook in hot oil about 2 min. per side.
Mushrooms (sliced)	Cover; cook in butter about 5 min.
Onions (cut in wedges)	25 to 30 min.
Parsnips (cut-up)	15 to 20 min.
Peas	10 to 12 min.
Potatoes (whole)	25 to 40 min.
Potatoes (quartered)	20 to 25 min.
Spinach	Cook in very small amount of water, 3 to 5 min.
Squash (summer, sliced)	5 to 10 min.
Squash (winter, cubed)	About 15 min.
Sweet potatoes	30 to 40 min.
Tomatoes (whole or cut up)	Cover tightly and cook without water, 10 to 15 min.
Zucchini (sliced)	5 to 10 min.

*A*sparagus is delicate in design, so it is advisable when buying this vegetable to choose firm, straight stalks with compact, closed tips. Asparagus will stay fresher if you wrap the stem ends in moist paper towels before refrigerating in a plastic bag.

Since this dish hints of the Far East, serve it alongside a platter of Peking Pork Chops & Rice (p. 67).

Asparagus & Tomato Toss

1	pound fresh asparagus	4	green onions, sliced on the bias into
1	tablespoon water		1-inch lengths
1	teaspoon cornstarch	1½	cups fresh sliced mushrooms
2	teaspoons soy sauce	2	medium tomatoes, cut in thin
¼	teaspoon salt		wedges
1	tablespoon cooking oil		

Snap off and discard the ends from the asparagus. Cut into 1-inch lengths, then wash. Blend water into cornstarch; stir in soy sauce and salt. Set aside.

Preheat a large skillet over high heat; add cooking oil. Add asparagus slices and green onions to hot oil and cook for 4 minutes. Add mushrooms; cook 1 minute more. Stir soy mixture; stir into vegetables. Cook and stir till thickened and bubbly. Add tomatoes and heat through. Serve immediately.

Serves 6

*F*or me, this recipe rates a "10"! It is not only tasty and elegant, but may be served with almost any main meal.

Asparagus Vinaigrette

1	pound fresh asparagus *or* 2 8-ounce	½	teaspoon paprika
	packages frozen asparagus spears	½	teaspoon dry mustard
2	tablespoons vinegar		Dash cayenne
2	tablespoons lemon juice	2	tablespoons snipped chives
½	cup vegetable oil	2	small tomatoes, chilled lettuce
2	teaspoons sugar		leaves
1	teaspoon salt		

Cut asparagus spears into 1-inch pieces. Place fresh asparagus in a skillet in a small amount of salted boiling water. Cover pan and cook till crisp-tender or about 8 to 10 minutes. (Or, cook frozen asparagus according to package instructions.) Drain. In a screw-top jar or bottle, combine vinegar, lemon juice, oil, sugar, salt, paprika, dry mustard, cayenne, and snipped chives. Cover and shake well. Arrange asparagus in a shallow dish; top with vinegar mixture. Cover and refrigerate for several hours or overnight, spooning vinegar mixture over asparagus occasionally.

To serve, drain asparagus, reserving vinegar mixture. Slice tomatoes. On each of 4 salad plates, arrange a few asparagus spears atop lettuce. Top each salad with a few tomato slices. Spoon a little of the reserved vinegar mixture over each salad.

Serves 4

T his salad makes a wonderful accompaniment for London Broil Marinade (p. 15) with Parsley New Potatoes (p. 156) and a hearty Burgundy.

Beets & Sour Cream Salad

1	pound beets	1	teaspoon sugar
1/2	cup sour cream	1/4	teaspoon salt
2	tablespoons milk		Dash of cayenne pepper
3	sliced green onions with tops	4	cups leaf lettuce
1	tablespoon vinegar		Optional: paprika

To prepare the beets, cut off all but 1 inch of the stems and roots; wash. In a covered pan, cook whole beets in boiling salted water until tender for about 35 to 40 minutes. Cool slightly and peel skin. Slice beets in round slices. Meanwhile, combine chilled sour cream, milk, onion, vinegar, sugar, salt, and cayenne. Mix thoroughly. Combine beets with the sour cream mixture and blend well. Chill for at least 1 hour in the refrigerator until cold. Place lettuce leaves in salad bowl. Spoon beet and sour cream mixture over the lettuce leaves and sprinkle with paprika, if desired.

Serves 4

*B*roccoli is successfully enhanced with a variety of sauces: try a cheese sauce, hollandaise, mayonnaise, or mustard sauce. Broccoli with cheese sauce is exceptional when served with Filet of sole or haddock.

Broccoli with Lemon Sauce

2 pounds fresh broccoli	1/2 teaspoon salt
1/2 cup chopped celery	Freshly ground pepper
1/2 cup green onion, chopped	1/2 teaspoon paprika
6 tablespoons butter *or* margarine	2 hard-cooked eggs, finely chopped
1/2 cup lemon juice	

Wash broccoli; remove outer leaves and tough part of stalks. Cut stalks into uniform spears. In covered pan, cook spears in a small amount of boiling salted water till crisp-tender, about 5 to 8 minutes. Drain well. In a small saucepan, cook the celery and green onion in butter until crisp-tender but not brown. Stir in lemon juice; heat through. To serve, layer broccoli and butter mixture in a serving dish. Add salt, pepper, and paprika and garnish with chopped egg.

Serves 8

*B*lack-eyed peas served over rice is a traditional dish served on New Year's Eve with all the fixin's: Finger-Lickin' Fried Chicken & Gravy (p. 26), Fried Sweet Potatoes (p. 153), and Down Home Greens & Ham Hocks (p. 150). Don't forget the hats and noisemakers!

Bull's-Eye Black-eyes

1 cup black-eyed peas	3 tablespoons butter
1 large onion, chopped	2-pound can tomatoes
1 clove garlic, minced	1 tablespoon Worcestershire Sauce
1 red pepper, cored, seeded, and chopped	1 teaspoon chili powder
1 green pepper, cored, seeded, and chopped	Salt and pepper to taste
	Cooked rice

Rinse black-eyed peas and place in a kettle with about 4 times as much water as peas. Cover pan; soak overnight. (Or, bring to a boil; simmer 2 minutes. Remove from heat. Cover; soak for one hour.) Do not drain. Cook until tender, for about an hour. Drain. Cook onions, garlic, and pepper in butter for about 5 minutes. Add tomatoes, Worcestershire sauce, chili powder, and salt and pepper, and simmer for 1 hour. Combine mixture with the peas and reheat. May be served with cooked rice, if desired. Serve very hot.

Serves 4

I keep saying someday I'll serve this at one of my next dinner parties. Maybe when I'm planning a Chinese menu. Fortune cookie say: "Someday not day of week!"

Buttered Green Beans & Water Chestnuts

1	pound green beans cut French-style	1/2	cup chopped green onions
1/4	cup melted butter *or* margarine		Pinch dried oregano, crushed
	5-ounce can sliced water chestnuts		

Wash and slice beans diagonally. In a covered pan cook French-style cut beans in a small amount of salted boiling water till crisp-tender, about 10 to 12 minutes. While beans are cooking, add butter or margarine to a skillet, and over moderate heat, cook the drained, sliced water chestnuts and green onions, until lightly browned, for about 5 minutes. Stir water chestnuts, green onions, and oregano into green beans. Serve immediately.

Serves 4

D id you know that Webster's Dictionary has three different meanings for the word "cabbage"? If you don't believe me, look it up!

Cabbage in Mustard Sauce

1	medium-size head of cabbage, cored and cut into wedges	1/2	teaspoon pepper
2	tablespoons chopped onion	1	cup milk
2	tablespoons butter *or* margarine	1	tablespoon prepared mustard
1	tablespoon flour	2	teaspoons prepared horseradish
1 1/2	teaspoons salt		Optional: parsley

In an uncovered pan, cook cabbage in a small amount of boiling salted water for the first few minutes, then cover pan and cook till crisp-tender, about 10 to 12 minutes. Drain well. Meanwhile, in a small skillet, cook onion in butter till tender. Blend in flour, salt, and pepper. Add milk, and stir till thickened. Add mustard and horseradish. Spoon sauce over cabbage wedges. Sprinkle with snipped parsley, if desired.

Serves 4

"Training is everything. The peach was once a bitter almond; cauliflower is nothing but cabbage with a college education."

Mark Twain

*"W*inter" *squash are acorn, banana, butternut, turban, Hubbard, and buttercup squash. Although squash can be peeled before cooking, it is* much easier to cook it first, and then remove the peel.

Candied Acorn Squash

2	acorn squash	2	tablespoons water
½	cup brown sugar		Salt and pepper to taste
½	cup butter *or* margarine		

Cut squash in half, discard seeds. In a large covered Dutch oven cook the halves in a small amount of boiling water until tender, about 45 to 50 minutes. In a saucepan combine brown sugar, butter, and water and cook till bubbly, stirring constantly. Spoon over squash, sprinkle with salt and pepper, and continue cooking for 10 more minutes.

Serves 4

*F*or color and texture, serve this sunny vegetable with Chicken on the Wild Side (p. 24) and a bowl of Chilled Herbed Mushrooms (p. 146). Fill the glasses with a frosty rosé and enjoy!

Carrots Lyonnaise

6	cups julienne carrots *or* carrot rounds	2	teaspoons cornstarch
¼	cup butter *or* margarine	½	teaspoon salt
3	medium-size onions, thinly sliced	¼	teaspoon ground ginger
2	tablespoons sugar	½	cup orange juice

Wash, trim and peel carrots. Place carrots in a saucepan containing a small amount of boiling salted water. Cover and cook till just tender, about 10 to 20 minutes. (About 10 minutes for the julienne strips and 20 minutes for the rounds.) Melt butter in a skillet over moderately low heat. Add onions and cook, stirring occasionally, until tender. Combine sugar, cornstarch, salt, and ginger in a small saucepan; gradually add orange juice. Place over moderately low heat and cook, stirring constantly, until mixture is thickened and smooth. Combine drained carrots, cooked onions, and orange sauce, tossing to coat evenly. Serve hot.

Serves 6 to 8

*A*n impressive dinner menu serves Halibut & Mushrooms in White Wine Sauce (p. 88) with the cauliflower and a basket of Fried Eggplant Straws (p. 152).

Cauliflower à la Polonaise

1 medium head cauliflower	1/4 cup fine dry bread crumbs
1 hard-cooked egg	1 tablespoon fresh parsley, snipped
1 tablespoon butter *or* margarine	

To prepare cauliflower, wash and remove leaves and woody stem. You can break the head into flowerets, if desired. In a covered pan, cook in a small amount of salted water till tender when fork-tested. Allow 20 minutes for a whole head and 10 to 15 minutes for flowerets. Cauliflower must be tested frequently when cooking, because the slightest overcooking will turn the vegetable dark, and it will become strong-flavored.

Chop hard-cooked egg. Heat butter or margarine till lightly browned; stir in crumbs, parsley and chopped egg. Spoon over cooked cauliflower.

Serves 5 to 6

*T*his vegetable works well when served with a fish dish—perhaps the Filet of Sole Veronica (p. 86) or the Trout Meunière (p. 90).

Cheesy Cauliflower

1 medium head cauliflower, broken into flowerets	1 cup milk
2 tablespoons butter *or* margarine	1 cup shredded sharp American cheese
2 tablespoons flour	1 teaspoon prepared mustard
1/4 teaspoon white pepper	1 tablespoon fresh parsley, snipped
1/4 teaspoon salt	

Wash cauliflower and remove leaves and woody stem. Break into flowerets. In a covered pan, cook flowerets in a small amount of boiling salted water for 10 to 15 minutes. Fork-test frequently for tenderness. Drain and keep warm.

Meanwhile, melt butter or margarine; blend flour, white pepper, and 1/4 teaspoon salt into butter. Add milk at once. Cook, stirring constantly, till thickened. Stir in cheese and mustard. Heat till cheese melts. *Do not boil.* Place flowerets on platter and spoon all of the cheese mixture over the cauliflower. Sprinkle with parsley.

Serves 6

*T*his very continental salad is chock-full of goodies and is delicious served with Veal Scaloppine Marsala (p. 136), lots of fresh French bread, and a bottle of Beaujolais.

Chilled Green Beans à la Niçoise

1	pound green beans, cut into 1-inch pieces	Dash of pepper
2	whole cloves	1 medium-size onion, thinly sliced
⅔	cup vegetable oil	1 medium-size green pepper, diced
¼	cup wine vinegar	2 medium-size tomatoes, quartered
½	teaspoon basil	2 cooked medium-size potatoes, quartered
½	teaspoon coriander	Optional: lettuce
⅛	teaspoon salt	

Cook green beans in a large pan in a small amount of salted boiling water; add cloves, and cook till beans are crisp-tender, about 20 to 30 minutes. Drain and cool. In a screw-top jar, combine oil, vinegar, basil, coriander, ⅛ teaspoon salt, and dash of pepper. Shake well. In a large serving bowl, place green beans, onion, diced green pepper, tomatoes, and potatoes. Pour herb mixture over vegetables and marinate for two hours. Toss. Salad may be served on lettuce leaves.

Serves 4

*M*ushrooms are highly perishable, and should be used at once. Cooked mushrooms add a special flavor to soups, and sautéed mushrooms make a great topper for burgers and steaks.

Chilled Herbed Mushrooms

1	pound mushrooms, sliced	3 tablespoons tarragon vinegar
½	cup olive oil	Dash dried tarragon, crushed
1	tablespoon grated onion	Dash dried thyme, crushed
1	tablespoon snipped chives	Few grains ground pepper
1	tablespoon chopped fresh parsley	Optional: lettuce
1	clove garlic, minced	
¾	teaspoon salt	

Wash and slice mushrooms. Combine remaining ingredients in a large screw-top jar, and shake well. Pour over sliced mushrooms, and refrigerate for at least 2 hours before serving. Stir the mushroom mixture and spoon on lettuce leaves, if desired.

Serves 4

T his cabbage salad is one of my favorites. It's super served on corned beef or pastrami sandwiches, or at a picnic with Sesame Seed Chicken Drummettes (p. 30), a platter of Spicy Spareribs (p. 72), Butterfry-Fly Shrimp (p. 110), and lots of cool drinks and cooler music.

Creamy Home Made Coleslaw

4	cups shredded cabbage	¼	cup white vinegar
1	cup carrot pieces, shredded with vegetable peeler	2	teaspoons sugar *or* to taste
½	cup sliced onion	½	teaspoon caraway seed
½	cup mayonnaise *or* salad dressing	¼	teaspoon salt

Combine shredded cabbage with carrot and onion. Blend together mayonnaise or salad dressing, vinegar, sugar, caraway seed, and ¼ teaspoon salt. Toss mayonnaise mixture with vegetables. Cover and chill.

Serves 8

O nions add flavor to many dishes and can be served in many different ways. For instance: shallots are most often chopped, and used as a seasoning. Small white onions and leeks are usually served in a cream sauce. Green onions work well in salads and in many Oriental dishes.

Creamed Onions

1	pound white pearl onions (small white onions)		Dash white pepper
3	tablespoons butter *or* margarine	1⅓	cups milk
2	tablespoons flour	1	cup shredded Muenster cheese
¼	teaspoon salt		Optional: parsley

In a covered pan, cook onions in small amount of salted boiling water, till nearly tender; about 15 to 20 minutes. Drain well. In a saucepan, melt butter; blend in flour, salt and white pepper. Add milk, cook and stir till thickened. Add shredded Muenster cheese; stir till melted. *Do not boil.* Stir in drained onions. Heat through. Garnish with parsley, if desired.

Serves 6

"What's the use of watching? A watched pot never boils."

Mrs. Gaskell

B *abies like this vegetable, and so did Popeye, so it's gotta be good.*

Creamed Spinach

2	10-ounce packages frozen, chopped spinach	1	cup light cream
3	tablespoons butter *or* margarine	1/2	teaspoon salt
2	tablespoons finely chopped onion	1/8	teaspoon ground nutmeg
2	tablespoons flour	1/2	teaspoon dried basil, crushed

Cook spinach according to package instructions. Drain thoroughly. Melt butter or margarine in a saucepan over moderately low heat; add onion and cook until tender, stirring occasionally. Remove from heat. Blend in flour; gradually add light cream. Cook over moderately low heat, stirring constantly, until thickened. Stir in salt, nutmeg, and basil. Pour sauce into drained spinach and heat gently, stirring occasionally.

Serves 6

W *hen cooking peas without another vegetable escort, it greatly helps the flavor to add 1/4 teaspoon of sugar to the cooking water. Dress up buttered peas with an herb or two for a fresh-tasting dish. Try marjoram, sage, or basil.*

Creamy Peas & Pearl Onions

1	cup whole pearl onions *or* 10-ounce package frozen small whole onions	1	tablespoon flour
		1/2	teaspoon salt
			Dash white pepper
2	cups shelled peas *or* 10-ounce package frozen peas	1	cup milk
1	tablespoon butter *or* margarine		Grated Parmesan cheese

In a covered saucepan, cook onions and peas in boiling salted water for about 10 minutes, or until tender. (If using frozen peas, add to onions only during the last 5 minutes.) Drain well.

Meanwhile, melt butter or margarine in saucepan over low heat. Blend in flour, salt, and white pepper. Add milk all at once; cook and stir till thickened. Pour over hot vegetables; stir to coat. Serve with Parmesan cheese.

Serves 4

*I*n appearance, this vegetable reminds me of a miniature head of lettuce, but in taste, it stands completely on its own. Serve with Braised Shoulder Lamb Chops (p. 41), Whipped Sweet Potatoes & Parsnips (p. 161), and for the salad, add a bowl of Marinated Cherry Tomatoes (p. 155).

Creamy-Style Brussels Sprouts

1 pound Brussels sprouts	$\frac{1}{2}$ teaspoon dry mustard
$\frac{1}{2}$ cup chopped onion	1 teaspoon salt
2 tablespoons butter *or* margarine	$\frac{1}{2}$ cup milk
1 tablespoon flour	1 cup sour cream
1 tablespoon brown sugar	

Trim Brussels sprouts' stems slightly and remove any wilted leaves; wash. Cut large sprouts in half lengthwise. Then, in a covered pan, cook sprouts in small amount of boiling salted water for about 10 to 15 minutes. Drain well. Meanwhile, in a medium-size skillet, cook chopped onion in butter or margarine till tender, but not brown. Blend in flour, brown sugar, dry mustard, and 1 teaspoon salt. Stir in milk. Cook, stirring constantly, till thickened. Blend in sour cream. Add cooked Brussels sprouts; stir gently to combine. Cook till heated through, but do not boil. Serve immediately.

Serves 6 to 8

*M*ake a big platter of Spicy Spareribs (p. 72), add a bowl of Bali-Hai Fried Rice (p. 76), plus this delicious curried salad, and you'll feel like you're on your own special island.

Curried Broccoli & Cauliflower Salad

$\frac{1}{2}$ pound broccoli	1 teaspoon curry powder
$\frac{1}{2}$ pound cauliflower	$\frac{1}{2}$ teaspoon dry mustard
$\frac{1}{2}$ cup milk	Dash of pepper
1 cup sour cream	3 medium tomatoes, cut into wedges
$\frac{1}{2}$ teaspoon seasoned salt	Lettuce

Wash vegetables and break into flowerets. In a covered pan, cook broccoli flowerets *only* in boiling salted water for about 5 minutes, until crisp-tender. Drain well. Combine milk, sour cream, seasoned salt, curry powder, dry mustard, and a dash of pepper. Mix cooled broccoli with cauliflowerets. Pour curry mixture over vegetables, stirring to coat. Cover and chill for two or three hours. Arrange broccoli and cauliflowerets and tomatoes on a bed of lettuce.

Makes 6 servings

*T*here is such variety in the greens family—turnip greens, collard greens, mustard greens, beet greens, dandelion greens, kale, chard, and Swiss chard . . . just toss 'em in a kettle, and be sure to cook 'em the same day you buy 'em for the best quality.

Down-Home Greens & Ham Hocks

1 pound mustard greens	1 medium-size onion, sliced
½ pound collard greens	1 jalapeño pepper, halved and seeded
½ pound turnip greens	1 tablespoon flour
4 cups water	¼ cup cold water
3½ pounds ham hocks	1 tablespoon hot sauce

To prepare the greens, wash them thoroughly in cool water to remove dirt and sand. Cut off any roots and remove damaged leaves and large mid-veins. Tear large leaves. In a large kettle, combine water and ham hocks; bring to a boil. Add onion, jalapeño pepper, mustard, collard, and turnip greens, and return to a boil. Reduce heat; simmer, covered, 1½ hours. Remove pepper. Dissolve flour in ¼ cup cold water and add to kettle, together with a few drops of hot sauce to taste. You may serve the greens in their juices separately from the ham hocks or together in a large serving bowl.

Serves 8

"How do they taste?
They taste like more."

H. L. Mencken

A *rtichokes are all at once fun to eat and a challenge. No other vegetable has such style.*

French-Dip Artichokes

4   artichokes
2   8-ounce containers French Onion
      dip with sour cream
2   tablespoons snipped parsley
½   cup finely chopped green onion

1   tablespoon lemon juice
1   teaspoon dried oregano, crushed
      Dash freshly ground pepper

To prepare: wash, trim stems, and remove any loose outer leaves. Cut off 1 inch of tops; snip off any sharp leaf tips. Place the artichokes in a large kettle and simmer in boiling salted water till a leaf pulls out easily. Cook for about 20 to 30 minutes. Drain on paper towels, upside down. Remove center leaves and chokes. Chill thoroughly.

Meanwhile, combine sour cream dip, parsley, green onion, lemon juice, oregano, and a dash of freshly ground pepper; chill well. Serve sauce with chilled artichokes.

Serves 4

T *he next best thing to a hamburger and french fried onion rings is a No-Risk Minute Steak (p. 17), served with Broccoli with Lemon Sauce (p. 142), plus the onion rings and a tossed green salad with a Roquefort dressing, and full glasses of Bordeaux.*

French Fried Onion Rings

2   Bermuda onions
1   cup all-purpose flour
1   teaspoon baking powder
½   teaspoon salt

1   egg, slightly beaten
⅔   cup milk
1   tablespoon vegetable oil
      Vegetable oil for frying

Cut off root ends of onions; peel and slice crosswise into ¼-inch slices. Separate slices into rings. Mix flour, baking powder, and salt together in a bowl. Add the egg, milk, and the 1 tablespoon oil; mix until smooth. Pour oil into a skillet or deep-fat fryer to a depth of 1½ to 2 inches. Heat oil, dip onion rings in batter, and place them, one at a time, in the oil. Cook rings until lightly browned on both sides. As rings brown, remove and drain on paper towels. Continue adding rings as room in skillet allows.

Serves 4 to 6

*T his Off-the-Top-of-My-Stove casserole dish is, in a word, classic! Since this
vegetable is so rich, a simple recipe (doubled) like Easy-Does-It Chicken
(p. 25) and a bowl of Risotto & Mushrooms (p. 82) will make your meal complete.*

French-Quarter Green Beans

1	pound green beans *or* 2 9-ounce packages frozen French-style green beans	½	teaspoon lemon zest
		½	teaspoon salt
			Dash pepper
1	tablespoon chopped parsley	½	cup milk
1	medium onion, sliced	1	cup sour cream
3	tablespoons butter *or* margarine	½	cup shredded cheddar cheese
2	tablespoons flour	¼	cup seasoned bread crumbs

To cut fresh beans French-style, slice diagonally. Cook cut beans in a covered
pan in a small amount of boiling salted water till crisp-tender, or about 10 to 12
minutes. (Or, cook frozen beans according to package instructions.) Drain.
Cook parsley and onion in 2 tablespoons of butter or margarine until onion is
tender. Blend in flour, lemon zest, ½ teaspoon salt, and a dash of pepper. Add
milk; cook and stir till thickened. Stir in sour cream and cooked beans; heat till
just bubbly. Sprinkle with cheese and bread crumbs. Add the remaining tablespoon of butter or margarine; cover for 1 to 2 minutes or until cheese melts.

Serves 8

*W hen choosing this pear-shaped vegetable, look for a firm, heavy-to-the-
hand eggplant with a dark, shiny, smooth skin, and a fresh-looking green
top. Eggplants may be stored in the refrigerator for up to two weeks.*

Fried Eggplant Straws

1	medium eggplant, peeled	2	tablespoons snipped parsley
1	slightly beaten egg	½	teaspoon salt
1	tablespoon water	⅛	teaspoon pepper
1	cup seasoned bread crumbs	½	cup cooking oil

Halve eggplant lengthwise, then cut crosswise into ½-inch slices. Cut slices
into ½-inch strips. Combine egg and 1 tablespoon water. Combine bread
crumbs, parsley, salt, and pepper. Dip eggplant strips in egg mixture, then in
bread crumb mixture. Cook eggplant in hot oil till tender and golden. Drain
on paper towels.

Serves 4 to 6

*I*s there really a difference between a sweet potato and a yam? What Americans eat are sweet potatoes. Yams are similar in taste and appearance but are found mostly in tropical climates.

Fried Sweet Potatoes

3	medium-size sweet potatoes	4	tablespoons butter *or* margarine
	All-purpose flour		Sugar

Wash potatoes and place in boiling water to cover. Cover pan and cook over moderate heat about 30 minutes, or until just tender. Remove potatoes from water, cool and then peel. Cut crosswise into ½-inch slices, and coat both sides with flour. Melt butter in skillet over moderate heat; add potatoes and cook until lightly browned on both sides. Sprinkle lightly with sugar.

Serves 4

*"Said Aristotle unto Plato,
'Have another sweet potato?'
Said Plato unto Aristotle,
'Thank you, I prefer the bottle.'"*

Owen Wister

*T*his basic and easy recipe goes great with your choice of any main dish, be it fowl, fish, beef, pork, or lamb; so, go ahead and surprise yourself!

Green Beans Amandine

1	pound green beans	1	teaspoon lemon juice
2	tablespoons butter		Freshly ground pepper
½	cup slivered almonds		

To cut fresh beans French-style, slice diagonally. Cook cut beans in a covered pan in a small amount of boiling salted water till crisp-tender, or about 10 to 12 minutes. Drain. Meanwhile cook slivered almonds in butter over low heat; stirring occasionally, until golden. Remove from heat; add lemon juice. Pour over beans. Dust with freshly ground pepper.

Serves 4

*T*his is great with any Italian-style main dish, such as Veal Parmigiana (p. 134) or Veal Piccata (p. 136), served up with side dishes of Vermicelli with Mushrooms & Prosciutto (p. 56), lots of warm bread and a bottle of soave.

Green Peppers Italiano

2 tablespoons vegetable oil	2 tomatoes, peeled and diced
2 large green peppers, cut into strips	1 teaspoon salt
1 medium-size onion, thinly sliced	1/4 teaspoon pepper
1 medium-size zucchini, cut into 1/2-inch slices	1/4 teaspoon dried basil, crushed
1/2 medium-size eggplant, peeled and cut into 1/2-inch slices	1 clove garlic, minced
	1 tablespoon chopped fresh parsley
	Optional: Parmesan cheese

Heat oil in a large skillet over moderate heat. Add pepper strips and onion; cook until just tender, about 5 minutes. Push peppers and onion to one side of skillet. Add zucchini and eggplant slices and cook until tender. (The eggplant will absorb most of the oil.) Add tomatoes, salt and pepper, basil, and garlic; stir gently to combine. Cover and cook over low heat about 10 minutes, or until tender-crisp. Sprinkle with parsley and Parmesan cheese, if desired.

Serves 4 to 6

*D*elete the cornstarch and butter from this recipe, and you will find you have made beets vinaigrette. (Be sure to chill all mixed ingredients for at least two hours.)

Harvard Beets

2 pounds fresh beets	1/4 cup beet liquid
1/3 cup sugar	1/4 cup vinegar
2 teaspoons cornstarch	1 tablespoon butter *or* margarine

Cut off all but 1 inch of the stems and roots of beets; wash. In a covered pan, cook whole beets in boiling salted water until tender for about 30 to 40 minutes. Drain. As soon as you can handle them, slip off the skin with your fingers. Cut into thin, crosswise slices. Mix sugar and cornstarch into a saucepan; stir in reserved beet liquid and vinegar. Cook over moderately low heat until thickened, stirring constantly. Add beets and butter and heat thoroughly.

Serves 4

T hese hashed-browns never miss! Just pass the Bloody Marys, and serve up this dish with any of the egg or frittata recipes you may think you'll have the most fun with.

Hashed-Brown Potatoes

1½ teaspoons salt	3 medium-size potatoes, cooked and diced
⅛ teaspoon pepper	
1½ tablespoons flour	2 tablespoons finely chopped onion
2 tablespoons milk	2 tablespoons vegetable oil

In a mixing bowl, combine salt and pepper with flour. Stir in milk and mix until smooth. Add potatoes and onion and stir thoroughly. Heat vegetable oil in a medium-sized skillet over moderate heat. Add the potato mixture and spread evenly, making one large cake that does not touch sides of the skillet. Cook until underside is brown. Cut into 4 squares, and turn pieces to brown other side.

Serves 4

F or these little red gems, just follow the recipe, place them on your buffet table in a lettuce-lined serving bowl, and watch them disappear.

Marinated Cherry Tomatoes

2 12-ounce baskets cherry tomatoes	½ teaspoon dried basil, crushed
⅔ cup vegetable oil	½ teaspoon dried oregano, crushed
¼ cup wine vinegar	1 teaspoon salt
¼ cup snipped parsley	¼ teaspoon pepper
¼ cup sliced green onion with tops	Optional: lettuce
½ teaspoon dried marjoram, crushed	

Wash and core tomatoes with vegetable peeler; place in a deep bowl. In a screw-top jar, combine oil, vinegar, parsley, green onion, marjoram, basil, oregano, 1 teaspoon salt, and ¼ teaspoon pepper. Shake well. Pour over tomatoes. Cover and refrigerate several hours or overnight, spooning herb mixture over tomatoes again. If desired, tomatoes may be served in lettuce-lined bowls.

Serves 6

*T**hese parsley potatoes are perfectly at home with a pot roast, any seafood recipe, or London Broil Marinade (p. 15), accompanied by either Creamy Peas & Pearl Onions (p. 148) or Creamy-Style Brussels Sprouts (p. 149).*

Parsley New Potatoes

1½ pounds new potatoes

6 tablespoons butter *or* margarine

1 tablespoon chopped fresh parsley

Scrub potatoes and peel a strip around the center of each potato. Place potatoes in a saucepan, and cover with boiling salted water. Cook over moderately low heat until potatoes are fork-tender, about 15 minutes. Melt butter in a saucepan over moderately low heat; stir in parsley. Heat and pour over drained potatoes.

Serves 4

Cooking time for boiling potatoes:

Whole potatoes	25 to 40 minutes
Quartered potatoes	20 to 25 minutes
New potatoes	12 to 15 minutes
Cubed potatoes	10 to 15 minutes

"The man who has nothing to boast of but his illustrious ancestors is like a potato—the only good belonging to him is underground."
Sir Thomas Overbury

T his recipe is pronounced ra-ta-too-eee, and I like to serve it (cut recipe in half) with Veal Cutlets Marinara (p. 131), and side dishes of hot Pasta with Butter & Cream (p. 50). Add a good Chianti and lots of hot buttered bread.

Ratatouille

⅓ cup olive oil	¼ cup chopped parsley
2 cups sliced onion	1 teaspoon salt
1 large clove garlic, pressed	Freshly ground pepper
1 medium-size eggplant, cubed and unpeeled	1 teaspoon dried tarragon, crushed
4 medium-size zucchini, thinly sliced and unpeeled	3 large tomatoes, cut into eighths
1 large green pepper, cored, seeded, and cut into 1-inch squares	Optional: Parmesan cheese

Heat oil in a Dutch oven over moderately low heat; add onion and garlic and cook until golden brown. Add eggplant, zucchini, green pepper, parsley, salt and pepper, and tarragon. Mix gently to coat with oil; if necessary, add a little more oil. Cover and cook 15 minutes. Stir in tomatoes; cover and cook 10 minutes longer or until vegetables are fork-tender. Sprinkle with Parmesan cheese, if desired.

Serves 8 to 10

W hen cooking red cabbage, always add a little lemon juice or vinegar to the water to prevent discoloring. This sweet and sour red cabbage recipe is perfectly matched with Tenderloin Tips & Noodles (p. 20) or 60-Minute Stroganoff (p. 9) and a bottle of Cabernet Sauvignon.

Red Cabbage in Wine

1	medium-size head red cabbage, finely shredded	1	teaspoon salt
4	tablespoons butter *or* margarine		Few grains pepper
2	tablespoons brown sugar	½	cup vinegar
		¼	cup dry red wine

Remove any outer leaves, wash cabbage, cut into wedges, and core. Shred wedges. Heat butter in a heavy saucepan over moderate heat. Add sugar, salt, pepper, and vinegar. Bring mixture to a boil and add cabbage. Cover and cook over moderately low heat, about 5 to 7 minutes, until tender but still crisp. Stir occasionally. Just before serving, stir in wine.

Serves 4

"S ummer" squash includes dark green zucchini, yellow crookneck, disk-shaped pattypan, and spaghetti squash. This variety of mild-flavored "summer" squash combines well with tomatoes, corn, and other vegetables.

Sautéed Zucchini

2	medium-size zucchini	½	cup butter *or* margarine
2	eggs, slightly beaten		Parmesan cheese
1½	cups seasoned bread crumbs		

Wash and cut zucchini into ¼-inch slices. Dip zucchini in beaten egg, then into bread crumbs to coat well on all sides. Melt butter in a large skillet over moderately low heat. Add zucchini slices in a single layer, and cook over moderately high heat until lightly browned on one side, about 2 minutes. Turn and brown lightly on the other side. Season to taste, and sprinkle with Parmesan cheese, if desired.

Serves 4

*C*orn is summer's golden harvest. When buying, look for fresh husks and choose ears of corn filled with even rows of plump kernels that spurt milk when pressed. For best results, refrigerate fresh corn in the husks.

South-of-the-Border Corn

1	large whole pepper, green or red		10½-ounce can tomatoes
½	cup butter *or* margarine	1	tablespoon Worcestershire sauce
½	cup finely chopped onion	1	teaspoon chili powder
1	clove garlic		Salt and pepper to taste
	17-ounce can whole-kernel corn		

Seed and finely chop pepper. Melt butter or margarine in a large skillet over moderate heat; add onion, garlic, and pepper and cook for about 5 minutes, or until almost tender. Add remaining ingredients; cover and simmer for 20 minutes over moderately low heat. Stir occasionally. Remove garlic clove and serve.

Serves 4

*T*his vegetable is a perfect accompaniment for such Oriental dishes as Beefy Black Bean Short Ribs (p. 10), Moo Goo Gai Pan (p. 29), Peking Pork Chops & Rice (p. 67), or Hocus-Pocus Pork Chow Mein (p. 73). So as fortune cookie say, "The choice is up to you!"

Spinach & Water Chestnut Toss

1	pound fresh spinach	½	teaspoon sugar
2	tablespoons cooking oil	½	cup sliced water chestnuts
2	tablespoons soy sauce	2	tablespoons chopped onions

Wash spinach thoroughly in sink filled with water. Repeat this process until all the sand is removed from the spinach. For the most flavorful spinach, cook vegetable in a few drops of water for 2 to 3 minutes. Turn leaves frequently while cooking. Drain well. Heat oil, soy sauce, and sugar in a skillet; add spinach, water chestnuts, and onion. Cook and toss till spinach is well-coated, and heated through, 2 to 3 minutes.

Serves 4

*T*his colorful recipe is a tasty treat served with Finger-Lickin' Fried Chicken
& Gravy (p. 26), or, for a change of pace, a Pasta Chicken-Curry Salad
(p. 61).

Summer Squash Medley

2	pounds yellow crookneck squash, thinly sliced	½	cup chopped celery
	10-ounce package frozen whole kernel corn	1	cube chicken bouillon
		⅓	cup water
1	red pepper, cored, seeded, and finely chopped	1	2½-ounce jar sliced mushrooms
		1	medium tomato
			Salt and pepper

In a covered pan, cook squash slices in a small amount of boiling, salted water.
Drain. In a saucepan, combine corn, pepper, celery, bouillon cube, and ⅓ cup
of water. Bring to a boil; reduce heat. Cover and simmer until vegetables are
tender, about 5 to 7 minutes. Drain mushrooms. Cut tomato into thin wedges.
Stir squash, mushrooms, and tomato wedges into corn mixture; heat through.
Season to taste with salt and pepper.

Serves 6

A delicious accompaniment to any main dish, or on a vegetarian platter with
Sauteed Zucchini (p. 158) and Broccoli with Lemon Sauce (p. 142), all
served on a bed of brown rice.

Sunset-Glazed Carrots

2	bunches small carrots, peeled	1½	tablespoons sugar, granulated or brown
¼	cup butter or margarine		
¼	cup orange juice	2	tablespoons Cointreau

Wash, trim and peel carrots. Leave tiny carrots whole, or, for larger carrots,
bias-slice them crosswise about ½-inch thick. Place carrots in a saucepan containing 1 inch of salted boiling water. Cover and cook till just tender, about 10
to 20 minutes. Meanwhile, in a small saucepan, melt butter over moderate
heat; add orange juice, sugar, and Cointreau. Cook, stirring constantly, till hot
and bubbly. Pour over hot carrots, tossing to coat evenly. Garnish with orange
twists, if desired.

Serves 6

T *his recipe is an unusual but flavorful way of preparing greens and is perfect accompanied by Sherried Country-Style Pork Ribs (p. 71) and a bowl of South-Of-The-Border Corn (p. 159). Serve a pitcher of mimosa punch, and listen to the wind in the willows.*

Sweet & Sour Greens

½ pound collard greens	1 tablespoon sugar
½ pound mustard greens	1 tablespoon cider vinegar
½ pound kale	¼ teaspoon salt
3 slices bacon	Freshly ground pepper
2 tablespoons flour	Optional: hot sauce
¾ cup hot water	

Wash greens and kale thoroughly in cool water to remove dirt and sand. Cut off any roots and remove damaged leaves and large mid-veins. Tear large leaves. In covered saucepan, cook greens and kale in a large amount of salted boiling water till tender, about 1 hour and 15 minutes. Drain well.

In a skillet, cook bacon till crisp. Remove bacon, reserving drippings in skillet. Blend flour into drippings. Add hot water, cook and stir till thickened. Stir in sugar, cider vinegar, salt, and pepper. Stir in drained greens and kale; heat through. Garnish with crumbled bacon, and a few drops of hot sauce, if desired.

Serves 4

T *his vegetable combination is exceptional with London Broil Marinade (p. 15) or Filet of Sole Amandine (p. 86). Add a plateful of Broccoli with Lemon Sauce (p. 142) and a tossed green salad with a creamy garlic dressing.*

Whipped Sweet Potatoes & Parsnips

1 pound sweet potatoes	Dash white pepper
1 pound parsnips	¼ teaspoon nutmeg
2 tablespoons butter	Optional: milk
½ teaspoon salt	2 sliced green onions

Wash sweet potatoes and parsnips, then scrape and remove outer skins. Slice potatoes and parsnips and place in a small amount of boiling salted water till tender, about 15 to 20 minutes. Drain. In a mixer bowl, combine hot vegetables, butter, salt and pepper, and nutmeg. Beat till smooth; add milk, if needed, to make fluffy. Top with green onions and more butter.

Serves 4 to 6

Herbs & Spices
The Basics

To preserve fresh herbs, you can chop them, place them in ice-cube trays, add a little water, and freeze. Transfer the cubes to a plastic bag, label it, and return it to the freezer. The next time you prepare soups or stews or spaghetti sauce, just drop in a cube or two.

Chives, basil, and parsley freeze especially well. Just wash and pat dry. Then mince and freeze in a plastic container.

Fresh ginger will keep for months stored in a plastic bag in the freezer. Just grate the amount you need, and return it to the freezer.

Ground chili powder, ginger, and paprika, once opened, should be kept in the refrigerator, as they lose their flavor quickly.

Try adding a half teaspoon of dried, crushed sage simmered with ground beef or pork in homemade or canned tomato sauce for an exceptional and flavorful sauce spooned over pasta.

When substituting dried herbs for fresh herbs in a recipe, use ⅓ the amount of fresh herbs required, and be sure to crush or crumble the dried herbs between the palms of your hands to release their flavor during cooking.

For a colorful as well as flavorful addition, try mixing paprika into the flour for coating a fish for frying. Also, sprinkle over cooked long-grain rice, or over fried potatoes prior to the cooking period.

Curried dishes are very zesty, but if you desire to make them a little more digestible, just cook the spices in the butter or oil first, then add the remaining ingredients.

Herbs

Suggested Uses

Basil   A member of the mint family with a strong affinity for tomatoes. Available in dried leaves or fresh.

Stews, shrimp Creole, fish chowders, spaghetti sauces, peas, eggplant, and tomatoes. ½ teaspoon leaves for 4 servings.

Bay leaf   The distinctively flavored leaf of the laurel tree. Available in whole, dried leaves.

Meats and poultry, halibut, salmon, shellfish, fish chowders, spaghetti sauces, tomatoes, and artichokes. 1 to 2 leaves for 4 servings.

Marjoram   A milder cousin of oregano. Present in Italian and poultry seasonings. Available dried and ground.

Meats and poultry, broiled fish, shellfish, eggs, lima beans, green beans, carrots, and zucchini. ½ teaspoon for 4 servings.

Oregano   "Wild marjoram." A perennial of the mint family, and an essential part of chili powder. Available dried and ground.

Meats and poultry, shellfish, cheese, eggs, spaghetti sauces, chili con carne, pizza, broccoli, and tomatoes. ¼ to 2 teaspoons for 4 servings.

Parsley flakes   A dried form of parsley. One of the mildest herbs.

Stews, soups, shellfish, salad dressings, omelets, potatoes, stuffings, and vegetables. 1 to 2 teaspoons for 4 servings.

Following are a few additional herbs that you may like to acquaint yourself with as you broaden your herb horizon.

Dill   Dill is fairly familiar because each time you eat a pickle, you're probably tasting dill in one form or another. Dill comes fresh, whole, powdered, and in dried leaves (called dill weed). This herb is especially good in potato salad and lentil soups. Also, it's quite wonderful with broiled fish and sliced cucumbers in a sour cream sauce. For 4 servings: use ⅛ to ½ teaspoon ground dill weed, ½ to 2 teaspoons whole seed, or 2 tablespoons fresh chopped leaves and stems.

Rosemary   As a culinary herb, rosemary has a sweet scent and a piney flavor. The fresh leaves make an aromatic garnish for chilled drinks or a fresh fruit cup. The freshly chopped or crumbled dry leaves may be used sparingly in sauces, stews, soups, and with lamb. Because rosemary has such a distinctive flavor, it should be used cautiously. For 4 servings, use ½ to 1 teaspoon dried leaves, or 1 to 2 teaspoons chopped fresh rosemary leaves.

Sage   Sage has a strong, fragrant odor. It is the basic ingredient in poultry seasoning, and is used in stuffings for poultry, meat, and fish. It is a perfect seasoning for pork. It comes in dried leaf form as well as ground and crushed or rubbed. For 6 cups of bread, use ¼ teaspoon of sage for stuffing.

Thyme   This is probably one of the most versatile herbs in the herb kingdom. It is used traditionally in New England fish chowders and is very popular in Creole dishes. It comes in leaf or ground form, and is moderately potent. Use ¼ to ½ teaspoon of leaf or ground thyme for a dish serving 6.

Mint   Fresh mint grows readily in home gardens. The leafy tops or crushed leaves make an edible garnish for all fresh fruits, beverages, ice cream, and gelatin desserts. Fresh or dried, mint gives a wonderful flavor to boiled carrots, peas, and boiled potatoes, and in jellied form makes a special treat when served with lamb and veal. For 4 servings: use ¼ to 1 teaspoon crushed dried mint or 1 to 2 tablespoons fresh, chopped mint.

Tarragon   This herb has a sweet, aniselike flavor, and must be used with discretion, and rarely with other herbs, for it will overpower them. It is especially comfortable in sauces, such as a hollandaise, mayonnaise, tartar, or mustard sauce, with fresh vegetables, fish, or poultry. Make a wonderful salad dressing with it: let ½ teaspoon dried tarragon leaves stand in ¼ cup French dressing for an hour before use on fresh salad greens. For other uses: for 4 servings, use ¼ to ½ teaspoon dried or ½ to 2 teaspoons chopped fresh tarragon.

"O cruelty, to steal my basil-pot away from me!"

John Keats

Spices

Suggested Uses

Cinnamon   Also called cassia. Available ground or in sticks.

Lamb and pork chops, beef stew, squash, broiled grapefruit, fruit pies, buns, mulled drinks, and coffee. $1/4$ to 1 teaspoon for 4 servings.

Cloves   The flower bud of the clove tree. Available whole or ground.

Ham, stews, gravies, squash, sweet potatoes, beets, fruit desserts, and spice cakes. (Eases the pain of a toothache, too.) $1/8$ to $1/2$ teaspoon for 4 servings.

Ginger   The spicy root of a tropical perennial. Available whole or ground.

Meats and poultry, carrots, sweet potatoes, chutney, pickles, and cookies. $1/4$ to 1 teaspoon for 4 servings.

Nutmeg   The inner kernel of the nutmeg fruit. The outer covering is called mace. Available whole or ground.

Meats, chicken, fish, carrots, cauliflower, spinach, stewed fruit, puddings, and eggnog. $1/8$ to 1 teaspoon for 4 servings.

Paprika   The pod of a sweet red pepper. Flavor varies from sweet to mildly pungent. Available ground.

Stews, chicken, fish, soups, shellfish, deviled eggs, potatoes, turnips, and salad dressings. 2 teaspoons to 2 tablespoons for 4 servings.

The preceding listing of spices is pretty basic. However, here are a few more which you may like to add to your collection:

Allspice   Not a blend of other spices, but quite a pungent berry. Its aroma is reminiscent of cinnamon, nutmeg, and cloves. It is used in fruit pies, cakes, cookies, and spiced fruit desserts.

Cayenne pepper   This is a golden-red member of the pepper family. It is always ground, and should be used with care because it's hot, hot, hot.

Saffron   This is a pungent spice, and a few strands of whole saffron will color a whole pot of rice. Saffron is dark-orange to reddish-brown in color and turns yellow when cooked. Saffron is expensive but a little goes a long way.

Tumeric   This is a deep yellow spice, and a relative of the ginger family. It is one of the spices usually used in prepared mustard and mustard pickles.

Blends

Suggested Uses

Chili powder   A blend of chili peppers, cumin seeds, oregano, garlic, and salt. Sometimes it includes cloves, allspice, and onion.

Chili con carne and many Mexican dishes. Hamburgers, seafood chowders, Spanish rice, corn, and bean salads. $1/4$ to 3 teaspoons for 4 servings.

Curry powder   A mixture that can include up to 20 spices, including allspice, black pepper, red pepper, cayenne, ginger, cinnamon, cardamom, coriander, mustard, saffron, and tumeric.

Curried meats and poultry, eggs, fish, shrimp, rice, tomatoes, creamed vegetables, lentils, salted nuts, and pickles. $1/4$ to 3 teaspoons for 4 servings.

"Variety's the very spice of life, that gives it all its flavor."

William Cowper

Index

INDEX

INDEX

INDEX